Pidgin
Grammar

An Introduction
to the Creole Language
of
HAWAI'I

Kent Sakoda and Jeff Siegel

3565 Harding Ave.
Honolulu, Hawai'i 96816
Phone: 1-800-910-2377
Fax: (808) 732-3627
www.besspress.com

Design: Carol Colbath
Index: Lee S. Motteler

Library of Congress Cataloging-in-Publication Data

Sakoda, Kent.
  Pidgin grammar : an introduction
to the Creole English of Hawaii / Kent
Sakoda and Jeff Siegel.
      p. cm.
  Includes glossary, bibliography,
index.
  ISBN 1-57306-169-7
  1. Pidgin English - Hawaii.
  2. Pidgin languages - Hawaii.
  3. Hawaiian language - Dialects.
  4. Creole dialects, English - Hawaii.
  I. Siegel, Jeff. II. Title.
  PE3625.S24 2003   427.95-dc21

Printed in the United States of America

To the memory of
Charlene J. "Charlie" Sato

Acknowledgments

Thanks go to Terry Crowley, Diana Eades, Ermile Hargrove, Vicki Knox, Terri Menacker, Amy Schafer, Al Schütz, Revé Shapard, and Ryo Stanwood for their helpful comments and suggestions on earlier drafts.

Contents

Introduction

This book is about the grammar of Pidgin. Ho! many people might be thinking: how can you have a grammar of Pidgin when it's not a language? Isn't it just "broken English"? The answer is that Pidgin IS a distinct language, and not just a "careless" form of English. True, most of the words in Pidgin come from English. But what makes it a separate language is that many of these words have meanings and functions different from those of English. Also, many of them are pronounced differently, and they are combined in ways not found in English. In other words, Pidgin has its own system of meanings, sounds and word combinations.

When people speak a language, they subconsciously know the "rules" for that language—that is, what words mean, how they are pronounced, and how they can be combined. In other words, they know what kinds of things you can say in the language, and what kinds of things you can't say.

For example, Pidgin speakers know that *grinds* means 'food' and *choke* means 'a lot of', even though these words don't have these meanings in English. They also know the meanings of words not found in English, such as *pilau* 'dirty' and *babooz* 'idiot'.

Pidgin speakers also know that the word for 'think' can be pronounced *tink*, 'that' as *dat,* and 'try' as *chry.*

And Pidgin speakers know that if you want to talk about something that happened in the past, you use the word *wen* before the action word, rather than adding *-ed*—for example: *I wen fix da car.* 'I fixed the car.'

Furthermore, Pidgin speakers know what word combinations are not acceptable in the language. For example, two words in Pidgin, *not* and *no,* are used to make sentences negative:

> *You not da boss.* 'You aren't the boss.'
> *My sister not skinny.* 'My sister isn't skinny.'

> *Da cat no stay in da house.* 'The cat isn't in the house.'
> *Joe no can play.* 'Joe can't play.'

Pidgin speakers know that people don't normally say *My sister no skinny* or *Joe not can play.* That's because like any other language, Pidgin has its own rules about what you can say, and what you can't say, and Pidgin speakers, like speakers of any language, subconsciously know these rules.

These days, linguists (people who study language) use the term "grammar" or "grammatical rules" to refer to the rules people know subconsciously for speaking their language. In the past, books on "grammar" were designed to teach people to talk in what was considered a "proper" or "correct" way. So, for example, English grammar books had rules such as "Do not end a sentence with a preposition." They would declare that "To whom did you speak?" (which few people would say nowadays) is correct, while "Who did you talk to?" (which most people would say) is incorrect. But nowadays, books about the grammar of a language simply describe the way people really talk, rather than prescribing how they *should* talk.

So this book, *Pidgin Grammar,* is about how people actually speak Pidgin. It is meant to be a resource for anyone who wants to find out about the language, and how it works. People who don't know anything about Pidgin will find this book useful, as will people who speak the language but may not have thought about its history or structure. We have tried to make the book as uncomplicated as possible and explain all linguistic terms and concepts as we go along. So the book is written for people without any background in linguistics, and for teachers who might find the explanations helpful for their students or themselves.

This book has six chapters. The first chapter is about the origins of Pidgin and its vocabulary. The second chapter is about the sound system of Pidgin and different ways of writing it. The next four chapters are about different types of words, phrases, and sentences in Pidgin and how they are combined. A short conclusion talks about some areas of future study regarding Pidgin, and about the issue of Pidgin in the classroom. At the end is a list of Pidgin words that come from English but have different functions or meanings, as well as Pidgin words that come from other languages.

We realize that this description of Pidgin is not complete, but we hope that it is accurate. Some Pidgin speakers might not agree with everything we have written, so we encourage readers to write to us with additions and corrections for the next edition.

Kent Sakoda: sakoda@hawaii.edu
Jeff Siegel: jsiegel@hawaii.edu

Chapter 1

The Origins and Use of Pidgin

1.1 The language and its names

"Pidgin" is spoken by an estimated 600,000 people in the state of Hawai'i in the United States, and by an unknown number of former Hawai'i residents in the other forty-nine states.

The name Pidgin is a shortening of the term "Pidgin English," which is how English speakers first referred to the form of speech that emerged in Hawai'i. They didn't recognize it as separate language but rather thought of it as a simplified or "broken" form of English. But, as we have seen in the introduction, although most of the vocabulary of Pidgin comes from English, it is a separate language.

The term "Pidgin English" has been applied to many different language varieties around the world that used English words but had their own grammatical rules, such as Pacific Pidgin English, West African Pidgin English, and Chinese Pidgin English. In fact, the word "pidgin" is thought to be derived from the Chinese pronunciation of the word "business."

Nowadays, the term "pidgin" has a different meaning in the field of linguistics. It refers to a new language that develops in a situation where speakers of different languages need to communicate but don't share a common language. This commonly happened on plantations, where people of several different language groups had to live and work together. In such situations, a particular language was used to run the plantations—for example, used by overseers in giving orders to the laborers. The laborers learned some words of the plantation language, but since they couldn't interact very much with speakers of that language, they didn't learn it fully.

When laborers from different language groups wanted to talk with each other, the only common means of communication they had were the words they'd learned from the plantation language. But when they used these words, they often changed the pronunciations, the meanings, and the ways the words were combined. These changes often reflected their own first

1

languages. Over time, people got used to using these words in certain ways, and the structure of a new language gradually formed. This kind of language is what we call a pidgin.

So, a pidgin takes its vocabulary (or lexicon) mainly from one particular language (called the "lexifier"), such as the plantation language, but it develops its own sound system, meanings, and structure, which are quite different from those of the lexifier. So it has its own grammatical rules.

Unlike other kinds of language, a pidgin is usually used only in limited circumstances—that is, for communication among people who speak different languages. It is learned only as a second or auxiliary language and not spoken as a first or native language.

In the early stages of its development, a pidgin appears to be simplified compared with its lexifier in terms of the amount of vocabulary and the kinds of grammatical structures. But later it may become more complex if it is used for more functions.

In Hawai'i, what we call Pidgin (with a capital P) first developed as a relatively simple pidgin language when people from Hawai'i, China, Portugal, Japan, Korea, the Philippines, and many other countries, worked together on the sugar plantations and needed some way to communicate with each other. The pidgin later began to be used for more functions outside the plantations and it became more complex. Some speakers started to use it not only with people from other language groups but also with members of their own families. Children in these families learned the pidgin at an early age and used it with other children who still spoke their parents' language at home. When this generation grew up, the pidgin became their dominant language and they passed it on to their own children. Gradually the pidgin became the mother tongue of most people born in Hawai'i.

Since the language was no longer spoken only as a second language with restricted functions, and now had a community of native speakers, it was by definition no longer a pidgin language. It had become what is called a "creole language" or a "creole." In everyday English, the term "creole" has a variety of meanings, ranging from 'the descendants of French, Spanish or Portuguese settlers in the Gulf states of America' to 'a kind of cooking'. But in linguistics, the term "creole" refers to a language that has developed from a pidgin but now is just like any other language in having a full range of functions, a complex grammar, and a community of native speakers.

So Pidgin in Hawai'i is actually a creole. Consequently, some people (especially teachers and linguists) also refer to Pidgin as "Hawai'i Creole English" or HCE for short. Other names used are Hawai'i English Creole and simply Hawai'i Creole.

Pidgin is just one of the many creole languages around the world. Perhaps the most well known is Jamaican Creole (called "Patwa" by its speakers), which is used in the lyrics of reggae music. Other creoles that have English as their lexifier language (but very different grammars from English and from each other) include Gullah (spoken on the islands off the coast of South Carolina and Georgia), Guyanese Creole (spoken in Guyana in northern South America), Kriol (spoken in northern Australia), and Krio (spoken in West Africa). Creoles with French as their lexifier are spoken in Louisiana, Haiti and other Caribbean islands, and Mauritius and other Indian Ocean islands. And creoles with Portuguese as their lexifier are spoken in Cape Verde Islands, Guinea-Bissau (West Africa), India, and Malaysia. There are also many other creoles with these lexifiers, and others with different lexifiers as well, including Arabic, Malay, and Ngbandi (a central African language). In total, an estimated 41.7 million people speak creole languages.

1.2 A detailed history of Pidgin

Now let's look at the history of Pidgin in more detail.

1.2.1 First contact

The Hawaiian Islands were populated by Polynesians some time between A.D. 200 and 400. The first Europeans to visit the islands were Captain Cook and his crew in 1778. At this time the native Hawaiian population numbered somewhere between 200,000 and a million. Contact with outsiders increased when Hawai'i became a stopover in the fur trade between China and the West Coast of North America from 1790 to 1810. Soon afterwards, the sandalwood trade and the whaling industry began, and during this time the foreign population in Hawai'i increased while the indigenous population decreased drastically because of introduced disease. In 1848 there were only approximately 88,000 Hawaiians left.

When the traders and whalers first came to Hawai'i, they needed to communicate in some way with the Hawaiians. They learned some of the Hawaiian language, and the Hawaiians learned some English. During this period some Hawaiians also began to work as sailors on foreign ships. No actual pidgin language had developed yet in Hawai'i, but various features of other English pidgins were used in communication. Some of these features are still found in Pidgin today, including *plenty* used to mean 'a lot of', *by and by* to indicate the future, *no* used before words to make them negative, and *got* (or *get*) meaning 'have'. These are illustrated in the following passages of the speech of Hawaiian sailors from Richard H. Dana's novel *Two Years Before the Mast*, published in 1840 (examples from Roberts 1998:14):

> Now got plenty money; no good, work. *Mamule* ['later'] money *pau* ['finished']—all gone. Ah! very good, work!— *makai hana hana nui* ['good work a lot']! . . . Aye! me know that. By -'em-by money *pau*—all gone; then *Kanaka* ['Hawaiian'] work plenty. . . . Aole! Me no eat Captain Cook!

The Hawaiian words *hana* 'work' and *pau* 'finished' are still used in modern Pidgin, especially in the phrase *pau hana* 'quitting time' or 'retirement'.

1.2.2 The first plantations and Pidgin Hawaiian

The first sugarcane plantation was established in 1835, and the expanding sugar industry led to the importation of laborers from many countries. About 2,000 Chinese plantation laborers arrived from 1852 to 1876, and more than 37,000 from 1877 to 1897. The majority were speakers of dialects of Cantonese, spoken in southern China. Approximately 2,450 laborers from Pacific islands were imported from 1877 to 1887—most from Kiribati (then the Gilbert Islands) but at least 550 from Vanuatu (then the New Hebrides), and some from Rotuma (currently part of Fiji), New Ireland and Bougainville (part of Papua New Guinea), and Santa Cruz (Solomon Islands).

More than 10,000 Portuguese workers were brought in from 1878 to 1887 and another 13,000 from 1906 to 1913. Nearly all of these were from the Madeira and Azores islands. Indentured laborers also came from continental Europe: 615 Scandinavians (mostly from Norway) in 1881 and 1,052 Germans from 1882 to 1885.

Steady Japanese indentured migration began in 1884, and by 1924 over 200,000 Japanese had arrived in Hawai'i. Migration from the Philippines began in 1907, and by 1930 over 100,000 Filipinos had come to Hawai'i. Other significant numbers of immigrants included 5,203 from Puerto Rico (1900–1901), 7,843 from Korea (1903–5), approximately 3,000 from Russia (1906–12), and about 2,000 from Spain (1907–13).

When the plantation era began, the Hawaiians were still in control of their islands, and their language was dominant. It was the language of government and of education for all non-European children, and it also became the language used to run the plantations. But many white plantation overseers did not learn Hawaiian fully, and the same was true of the imported Chinese laborers. A new form of language began to be used for communication among whites, Chinese, and Hawaiians—with words mostly from Hawaiian but with pronunciation, meanings, and structure different from Hawaiian. When laborers started coming from Portugal and other countries in the 1870s, this new language consolidated on the plantations. So the first real pidgin in Hawai'i was Pidgin Hawaiian, not Pidgin English.

Pidgin Hawaiian differed from real Hawaiian in many ways. In pronunciation, the "glottal stop" (a sound produced by suddenly blocking the flow of air in the voice box) was not used in some words. (This sound is represented by the 'okina (') in Hawaiian.) For example, pi'i mai was pronounced pi mai. This expression meant 'to come' in Pidgin Hawaiian, but it means 'to climb in this direction' in real Hawaiian. Other words changed their meaning as well—for example: hapai 'to bring' (originally 'to carry') and makana 'to give' (originally 'gift'). Some words changed their form—for example: hana hana 'work' (from hana) and nuinui 'many, much' (from nui and nunui). Words derived from other languages were also used, such as pihi 'fish' (from English, but with Hawaiian pronuncation) and kaukau 'food, eat' (from Chinese Pidgin English chow chow).

The way words were combined also differed in Pidgin Hawaiian, as shown in this quotation from the criminal court testimony of a Japanese immigrant in 1892 (from Roberts 1995:41):

Kela lio oe hele hauhau lela palani wau ma ka ponei.
(Literally: 'That horse you go eat that bran I in the last-night.')
'Your horse went to eat my bran last night.'

In Hawaiian this would be:

Ua hele kou lio e 'ai i ka'u palani i ka pō nei.

You can see several differences here. First, the small word *ua* is missing in the pidgin. In Hawaiian this shows the event had already taken place. Second, possession is shown in the pidgin by the word meaning 'you' or 'I' following the thing possessed (*lio oe* 'horse you' and *palani wau* 'bran I'), but in Hawaiian it is shown by words meaning 'your' and 'my' preceding (*kou lio* 'your horse' and *ka'u palani* 'my bran'). The order of the other words is also different—in Pidgin Hawaiian it's *horse your went* but in Hawaiian it's *went your horse*.

1.2.3 The development of Pidgin English

The change from the dominance of Hawaiian to the dominance of English began in 1875, when the Reciprocity Treaty with the United States was signed. This allowed free trade and a greater influx of Americans. Also the number of Hawaiians continued to decline and by 1878, the number had decreased to fewer than 50,000. In the decade from 1878 to 1888, there was a dramatic increase in the number of English-medium schools and a decrease in the number of Hawaiian schools. At the same time, Chinese and Portuguese families began to arrive, whereas previously most of the laborers had been single men. This meant that there was an increased number of children being exposed to English in the now English-medium public schools, including substantial numbers from the first generation of locally born children of immigrants.

During this period, English also began to gradually replace Hawaiian as the language of the plantations, and as a result an English-lexified pidgin (or Pidgin English) began to develop. At this stage, many people used a mixture of Pidgin Hawaiian and some words from English, as in this example, in which the English words are underlined:

Oe no tumach holoholo, hausu stop, mama nana.
(Literally: 'You no too-much travel-around, house stop, mother look.'
'Don't go out so much. Stay home and take care of your mother.'
(Bickerton and Wilson 1987:70)

Mi no pilikia but nuinui hanahana nuinui kala.
(Literally: 'Me no trouble but plenty work, plenty money.')
'I'm not troublesome, but I'm making a lot of money.'
(Roberts 1993:3)

These examples show some features that became part of the Pidgin English that was developing: *too much* used to mean 'a lot (of)' or 'very', *stop* meaning 'stay or live at', and *me* used for 'I'. They also show one of the features from the early 1800s: *no* as a negative marker.

The mixture of Pidgin Hawaiian and English led to many Hawaiian words coming into the early Pidgin English as well, especially those concerning the plantations, such as *hana hana* 'work' in the example above, and others such as *hapai ko* 'to load cane', *hanawai* 'to irrigate' and *hoehana* 'to hoe'. Some nonplantation words are still found in modern Pidgin, for example, *pilikia* 'trouble', as in the example above.

At first, mainly on the plantations, people combined words of English origin (and some of Hawaiian origin) in all kinds of ways that differed from English. But in the last few years of the nineteenth century, certain patterns became more accepted, and people started saying things in similar ways, so that a new structure emerged. It was then that Hawai'i Pidgin English (sometimes called HPE) became established as a new auxiliary language.

At the beginning of the twentieth century, HPE began to be used more and more for communication between ethnic groups outside the plantations, especially in the mixed urban areas. An important factor was the emergence of large numbers of the first generation of locally born Japanese, who came into the public schools and learned HPE from their classmates. (It must be remembered that most standard-English-speaking children were attending private schools.) As children grew older, many of them spoke HPE more than their mother tongue, so it became their "primary language"—that is, the language they used most.

A play by Kathryn Bond (1937) presents a fictional example of HPE as it was spoken by the Chinese. In the scene below, two old men are sawing firewood.

Lim Sui: Wassa matta you lazy ol' Pake? Hully up; pull mo' fas'.

Wing Bo: Mo' fas' no goo'. You allee time like hully up. Wassa matta you?

Lim Sui: No mo' wood, no can cook licee. Hully up.

Wing Bo: Slow kine all ligh'. Bymby pau. (Grunts)

Lim Sui: You no hully up saw wood, me no can cook.

Wing Bo: No tlouble—tomollow kaukau all ligh'. No need hully up. (Grunts and stops sawing) You see John Pake?

Lim Sui: No see um.

Wing Bo: Nisee Pake no goo' wife got. Wassa matta? John Pake allee same me fitty year, sitty year stop Kohala. Wassa matta no get um Pake wife? Pololican wife no goo'. Me come Kohala, stop Kohala fitty, sitty year, no one time see nother waihini goo' all same Pake wife.

Translation:

Lim Sui: What's wrong, you lazy old Chinaman. Hurry up, pull faster.

Wing Bo: Faster isn't good. You always want to hurry. What's wrong with you?

Lim Sui: If there's no wood, I can't cook rice. Hurry up.

Wing Bo: Slow is all right. It'll be finished soon. (Grunts)

Lim Sui: If you don't hurry up sawing the wood, I won't be able to cook.

Wing Bo:	No trouble—eating tomorrow is all right. No need to hurry. (Grunts and stops sawing) Did you see John Pake?
Lim Sui:	I didn't see him.
Wing Bo:	This Chinaman has a no good wife. What's the matter? John Pake just like me has lived in Kohala fifteen or sixteen years. Why doesn't he get a Chinese wife? A Puerto Rican wife is no good. I came to Kohala and stayed fifteen or sixteen years, but I've never seen any other woman as good as a Chinese wife.

The passage shows several features of HPE that are not found in modern Pidgin. Some of these reflect the influence of the Chinese speakers' first language: the use of the 'l' sound in place of 'r' (*hully, licee, ligh'*), leaving the last sound off words (*goo', ligh'*), adding -*ee* on the end of words (*allee* 'all', *licee* 'rice'). Other features of HPE (but not modern Pidgin) were found more generally: the use of *allee same* (or *all same*) to mean 'like', ending the sentence with *got, stop* meaning 'stay or live at'. Many other features, however, are still found in Pidgin: *pake* 'Chinese person', the pronunciation of fast as *fas'*, *mo' fast* 'faster', *no mo'* 'there isn't any', *like* 'want' *no can* 'can't', *kaukau* 'food, eat', *bymby pau* 'finish soon', *um* used instead of 'him, her, it, or them', and the Hawaiian word *wahine* 'woman' (here *waihini*).

1.2.4 The emergence of modern Pidgin

At the turn of the century, the second generation of locally born Chinese and Portuguese began to appear on the scene. By this time most of their parents were bilingual in their traditional language and Pidgin English (HPE), and many used this pidgin as their primary language. So in many cases, parents spoke to their newborn children in HPE, rather than in Cantonese or Portuguese. The result was that many of this second generation of immigrants acquired HPE as their first language.

At the same time, many Hawaiians had intermarried with Chinese and other immigrants and had children. (The census of 1910 gave the figures of 26,041 Hawaiians and 12,506 Part-Hawaiians.) It is likely that for many of these interethnic marriages, the language of the home was HPE, so that many of the Part-Hawaiian children also learned HPE as their first language.

Since HPE was now spoken as a first language, it was technically no longer a pidgin language, but rather a creole. So it was at this time that we can say that Hawai'i Creole, or modern Pidgin, began to emerge. Most linguists agree that Pidgin was established as a distinct language some time between 1905 and 1920, as more and more second-generation locally born Chinese and Portuguese—later joined by larger numbers of locally born Japanese—acquired it as their first language. Some time between 1920 and 1930, the number of locally born children of immigrants grew to equal the number of foreign born, and it can be said that this was the time that Pidgin became fully established as the language of the majority of the population of Hawai'i (see Roberts 2000).

As we have seen, many of the features of HPE came into modern Pidgin. Other HPE features were also found in earlier Pidgin, but have dropped out as the language changed over the years. For example, an article in the *Hawaii Educational Review* of September 1921 gives some features of the "Pidgin English" (by then, actually a creole) used by school students. Below are some examples of what the article called "incorrect," with the "correct" forms given. The old Pidgin features are shown in bold. (Of course, linguists would not agree that structures in Pidgin or any other language are "incorrect" just because they are different from standard English.)

*I **stop** Honolulu.*	'I live at Honolulu.'
*I **no got** pencil.*	'I don't have a pencil.'
*Him **blow** my head.*	'He hit my head.'
*He been **push** my hair.*	'He pulled my hair.'
***What for** you talk like that?*	'Why do you talk like that?'
*I **too much** like that one.*	'I like that one very much.'
***Suppose** rain, I no can go.*	'If it rains, I cannot go.'
*He look **all same** chicken.*	'He looks like a chicken.'
*This is **she's** book.*	'This is her book.'
*John go **catch** grass.*	'John has gone to get grass.'

On the other hand, many of the other features listed as "incorrect" forms in the article are still found in modern Pidgin. These are described later in this book.

Although there were many similarities between the newly emerged creole that became modern Pidgin and its Pidgin English predecessor, there were also many differences. For one thing, the creole did not have the variation in pronunciation that was caused by influences from other languages in the pidgin. Also, many grammatical features emerged in the creole that were not found in the earlier pidgin. So, for example, the following features of modern Pidgin were not found in the earlier Pidgin English:

the use of *never* to show that something did not occur in the past;

the use of *stay* to show a continuing action; and

the use of *for* in place of *to*.

These were also mentioned in the 1921 article in the *Hawaii Educational Review*:

I **never** *do like that.*	'I did not act in that way.'
I **stay** *working my house.*	'I was working at home.'
We are ready **for** *play ball.*	'We are ready to play ball.'

1.2.5 Influence of other languages

We have already seen that many words from Hawaiian came into modern Pidgin through Pidgin Hawaiian and Pidgin English. But the structure of Hawaiian has also affected the structure of Pidgin, making it different from that of English. One example is word order. In Hawaiian, there are sentences such as *Nui ka hale*. Literally this is 'Big the house', which in English would be 'The house is big'. Similarly, in Pidgin we find sentences such as *Big, da house* and *Cute, da baby*.

Another example is expressions from Hawaiian such as *Auwē, ka nani!*, which is literally 'Oh the pretty!' meaning 'Oh, how pretty!'. Similarly, in Pidgin we find the same kind of expression—for example, *Oh, da pretty!* and *Oh, da cute!*

Other languages have affected the structure of Pidgin more than the vocabulary. One such language is Cantonese. For example, in Cantonese the word *yáuh* means both 'have/has' and 'there is/are', as in these sentences:

*Kéuihdeih **yáuh** sāam-go jái.* 'They have three sons.'
(they *yáuh* three sons)

***Yáuh** go hahksāang hóu síng.* 'There's a student who's very bright.'
(*yáuh* a student very bright)

Similarly, in Pidgin the word *get* is used to mean both 'have/has' and 'there is/are', as in these sentences:

*They **get** three sons.* 'They have three sons.'

***Get** one student he very bright.* 'There's a student who's very bright.'

Portuguese appears to have affected the structure of Pidgin even more. For instance, Portuguese uses the word *para* meaning 'for' in some places where English uses *to*, as in this sentence:

*Carlos é homem **para** fazer isso.* 'Charles is the man to do that.'
(Charles is man for do that.)

Similarly, *for* (or *fo*) is used in Pidgin:

*Charles is da man **fo** do 'um.* 'Charles is the man to do it.'

Also in Portuguese, the word *estar* (with various conjugations, such as *está*) has several different functions, as in these examples:

*O livro **está** sobre a mesa.* 'The book is on the table.'
(the book *está* on the table)

*A água **está** fria.* 'The water is cold.'
(the water *está* cold)

*João **está** escrevendo uma carta.* 'John is writing a letter.'
(John *está* writing one letter)

A casa está construida. 'The house is finished.'
(the house *está* constructed)

In Pidgin, the word *stay* has the same functions:

Da book stay on top da table. 'The book is on the table.'

Da water stay cold. 'The water is cold.'

John stay writing one letter. 'John is writing a letter.'

Da house stay pau already. 'The house is finished.'

The pronunciation of Pidgin also has some similarities to Hawaiian, Cantonese, and Portuguese—especially in vowel sounds (section 2.1.2) and intonation in questions (section 2.5.4), but these connections have not been studied in any detail.

So the ethnic groups whose languages most influenced the structure of Pidgin seem to have been the Hawaiians, Chinese and Portuguese. But the influence of the Hawaiians declined steadily as their numbers declined and the numbers of other ethnic groups increased. By 1900, there were more Portuguese and Chinese than Hawaiians and Part-Hawaiians. Even though the Japanese were by far the largest immigrant group, their language appears to have had little effect on the structure of Pidgin. One reason for this was first suggested by the famous Pidgin scholar John Reinecke, who wrote (1969:93): "The first large immigration of Japanese did not occur until 1888 when the Hawaiian, Chinese, and Portuguese between them had pretty well fixed the form of the "pidgin" [English] spoken on the plantations."

Another reason is that, as we have seen, it was the locally born members of immigrant groups who learned Pidgin English as their primary or first language and therefore affected the development of the creole that became modern Pidgin. When the creole first began to emerge, the locally born population was dominated by the Chinese and Portuguese. Of these two groups, the Portuguese were the more important. In 1896, they made up over half of the locally born immigrant population. For the Portuguese, the number of locally born came to equal the number of foreign born in

1900, whereas this did not occur for the Chinese until just before 1920, and for the Japanese, not until later in the 1920s (see Roberts 2000).

The Portuguese were also the most significant immigrant group in the schools. They were the first group to bring their families, and their demands for education for their children in English rather than Hawaiian were partially responsible for the increase in English-medium public schools. From the critical years from 1881 to 1905, Portuguese children were the largest immigrant group in the schools, with over 20 percent from 1890 to 1905.

Another factor was that the Portuguese, being white, were given a disproportionate number of influential positions on the plantations as skilled laborers, clerks, and lunas ('foremen') who gave orders to other laborers. In fact, the number of Portuguese lunas was three times larger than that of any other group.

The Portuguese community was also the first to shift from their traditional language to Pidgin. By the late 1920s, the Portuguese had the lowest level of traditional language maintenance, and the greatest dominance of English or Pidgin in the homes, followed by the Hawaiians, and then the Chinese (see Siegel 2000).

But that is not to say that Japanese has had no influence on Pidgin. As we will see in the next section, many Japanese words have come into the language, and several Pidgin expressions, such as *chicken skin* 'goose bumps', are direct translations of Japanese. Also, the way many "discourse particles" are used—such as *yeah* and *no* at the end of a sentence (see sections 3.14 and 5.10)—seems to be due to Japanese influence. Furthermore, the structure of narratives in Pidgin is very similar to that of Japanese (see Masuda 2000).

1.3 Pidgin vocabulary

The vast majority of words in Pidgin are derived from English, and have the same meanings as their English counterparts. However, many Pidgin words have changed in meaning or have additional meanings—for example:

alphabet	'alphabet, letter of the alphabet'
lawnmower	'lawnmower, to mow' (e.g., *lawnmower the grass*)

package	'package, sack, paper bag'
pipe	'pipe, faucet'
panty	'panty, sissy, weakling'
pear	'pear, avocado'
off	'off, turn off' (e.g., *off the light*)
broke	'broke, broken, break, torn, tear, tore' (e.g., *He broke my shirt.*)
shame	'shame, shy, bashful, embarassed'

Other words and expressions are derived from English but have changed in form, and in some cases in meaning as well:

cockaroach	'cockroach, to steal or sneak away with'
bafe	'bathe'
brah (bla, blala)	'brother'
boddah	'bother'
fut	'fart'
mento	'mental, insane'
nuff	'enough'
hybolic	'using fancy (or standard-sounding) language'
garans	'guaranteed'
laters	'see you later'
whatevahs	'whatever, it doesn't matter'

There are also many compounds and expressions made up of English-derived words, but not found in English—at least not with the same meaning:

buckaloose	'go out of control'
bulai	'to tell lies' (bull + lie)
bolohead	'bald' (bald + head)
buddha-head	'local person of Japanese ancestry'
howzit	'greeting, how are you?'
cat tongue	'unable to drink or eat hot things'
catch air	'breathe'
chicken skin	'goose bumps'
stink eye	'dirty look'

talk stink	'say bad things about someone'
talk story	'have informal conversation, tell stories'
broke da mouth	'very delicious!'

In addition, Pidgin has many words derived from other languages. The largest number of such words (over one hundred) come from the Hawaiian language. Many of these have come into the English spoken in Hawai'i as well. Some examples are:

akamai	'smart'
haole	'white person (European)' (Hawaiian *haole* 'foreigner')
hapai	'carry, pregnant' (Hawaiian *hāpai*)
huhu	'angry, offended' (Hawaiian *huhū*)
imu	'earth oven'
kapakahi	'crooked, inside-out'
keiki	'child, children'
koa	'kind of native forest tree'
kokua	'help' (Hawaiian *kōkua*)
lanai	'verandah' (Hawaiian *lānai*)
lei	'flower garland'
lilikoi	'passion fruit' (Hawaiian *liliko'i*)
lolo	'stupid, crazy' (Hawaiian *lōlō*)
mahimahi	'dolphin fish'
manini	'stingy, undersized'
ohana	'extended family' (Hawaiian *'ohana*)
okole	'buttocks' (Hawaiian *'ōkole*)
ono	'delicious' (Hawaiian *'ono*)
opala	'trash, rubbish' (Hawaiian *'ōpala*)
pau	'finish, finished'
pilau	'dirty'
pilikia	'trouble, bother'
puka	'hole, perforation'
pupu(s)	'party snacks, finger food' (Hawaiian *pūpū*)
wahine	'woman'

Japanese has also provided many words to Pidgin (approximately forty), but some of these are used primarily by people of Japanese ancestry. Some examples are

bachi	'punishment, retribution'
bento	'Japanese-style box lunch'
bocha	'bath, bathe' (Hiroshima/Yamaguchi dialect)
chichi(s)	'breast(s)' (Japanese *chichi* 'milk')
daikon	'kind of turnip'
janken po	'paper, scissors and stone game' (Japanese *jaken pon*)
mochi	'rice patty'
musubi	'rice ball' (Hiroshima/Yamaguchi dialect)
nori	'dried seaweed'
obake	'ghost'
shishi	'urine, urinate' (Japanese *oshikko*)
shoyu	'soy sauce'
tako	'octopus'
ume	'partially dried salted sour plum pickle'
zori(s)	'rubber thong(s), flip-flop(s)' (Japanese *zori*)

In addition, Pidgin has words from Portuguese and other languages—for example:

malassada	'kind of doughnut' (Portuguese)
babooz	'idiot' (Portuguese *babosa* 'stupid, simpleton')
li hing mui	'salty, sour dried plum' (Chinese languages)
char siu	'barbequed pork' (Chinese languages)
adobo	'Filipino dish with pork or chicken cooked in vinegar and garlic' (Filipino languages)
bago-ong	'Filipino fermented fish sauce' (Tagalog)
kimchee	'Korean spicy pickled cabbage' (Korean)
lavalava	'sarong' (Samoan)
kaukau	'food' (Chinese Pidgin English *chow chow*)

Finally, there are some compounds, blended words, and expressions made up of words from English and other languages—for example:

haolefied	'become like a white person' (Hawaiian *haole* ' foreigner')

onolicious	'delicious' (Hawaiian *'ono* 'delicious')
hanabata	'snot' (Japanese *hana* 'nose'; *bata* from English *butter*)
hele on	'move on' (Hawaiian *hele* 'go, come, move')
hulihuli chicken	'chicken barbecued on a spit' (Hawaiian *huli* 'to turn')
kalua pig	'pig baked in a ground oven' (Hawaiian *kālua* 'bake in ground oven')
kukui nuts	'candlenuts' (Hawaiian *kukui* 'candlenut tree')
poi dog	'mixed breed dog' (Hawaiian *poi* 'pounded taro')
chawan cut	'haircut shaped like an inverted rice bowl' (Japanese *chawan* 'rice bowl')
daikon legs	'white, short, and fat legs' (Japanese *daikon* 'a kind of turnip')
buta kaukau	'pig slop' (Japanese *buta* 'pig', Pidgin *kaukau* 'food')

Additional words and expressions from English with different meanings and words from other languages can be found in the word list at the end of this book.

1.4 The current situation

Since its development, Pidgin has been used mostly as the informal language of families and friends, and has been considered an important badge of local identity—i.e., the language of people born and bred in Hawai'i, especially ethnic Hawaiians and descendants of plantation laborers. Attitudes toward the language have always been ambivalent. While recognized as being important to local culture, it has at the same time been denigrated as corrupted or "broken" English, and seen as an obstacle to learning standard English, the official language of the schools, government, and big business.

But in recent years, there has been a great deal of advocacy for Pidgin, resulting in changing attitudes and use in wider contexts. The turning point may have been in 1987, when the Hawai'i Board of Education attempted to implement a policy that allowed only standard English in the schools. Instead of being well received by the community, the policy evoked a strong negative reaction from parents, teachers, university faculty, and other community groups. The policy was seen as discriminatory, and as an unfair attack both on Pidgin and on local culture in general. (See the work of Charlene J. Sato, especially 1989, 1991.) The debate generated many letters to local newspapers and much discussion on radio and television, the majority strongly supporting Pidgin. Similar debates have erupted since then (the most recent in 1999 and 2002), as educational administrators and some members of the public seek to blame Pidgin for poor state results in national standardized tests in reading and writing.

Since 1998, a group of people, mainly from the University of Hawai'i at Mānoa, have been meeting regularly to discuss linguistic, social, and educational issues concerning Pidgin. This group is called "Da Pidgin Coup" (all puns intended). Following the public debate in 1999, the group wrote a position paper, "Pidgin and Education," as a basis for discussions with education officials and teachers, and for public education efforts as well. The aim was to provide information, backed up by research, about the complex relationship between Pidgin and English, and about the equally complex issues surrounding the use of Pidgin in education. (The position paper can be seen on the web at <www.hawaii.edu/sls/pidgin.html>.)

The domains in which Pidgin is used have also been expanding in recent years to include published works. *Pidgin to da Max* (Simonson, Sakata and Sasaki 1981) and its sequel *Pidgin to da Max Hana Hou* (Simonson et al. 1982) are entertaining descriptions of the language itself, and have sold more than 200,000 copies. The establishment of Bamboo Ridge Press in 1978 stimulated local writing, and over the past two decades, there has been a dramatic increase in the publication of short stories, plays, poetry, and novels unique to Hawai'i. Some of the most notable authors using Pidgin are Eric Chock, Lisa Kanae, Darrell Lum, Milton Murayama, Ed Sakamoto, Gary Pak, Lee Tonouchi, and Lois-Ann Yamanaka—just to name a few. The most remarkable extension of use of the language has been in the translation of the New Testament (*Da Jesus Book*), published in 2000. Over 11,000 copies were sold in the first year it appeared. (See <www.pidginbible.org>.)

Nevertheless, Pidgin remains primarily a spoken language, and it is spoken in a variety of ways. Some people speak "heavy" or "strong" Pidgin, which is very different from English. (Linguists call this form the "basilect.") Other people speak a "lighter" form of Pidgin, which is close to standard

English. (This is called the "acrolect.") The majority of speakers speak varieties in between (the "mesolects") and can switch back and forth between lighter or heavier forms of Pidgin as required by contextual factors such as who they're talking to, topic, setting, and formality. Many speakers are also completely bilingual and can switch between Pidgin and a form of standard English.

There is a widespread belief that this variation in the way Pidgin is spoken is a result of a gradual change taking place whereby Pidgin is becoming more and more like English. However, there's evidence that such variation existed from the earliest days of the language. Furthermore, the desire to project a separate local identity will most likely ensure that the language remains distinct from English. Nevertheless, there is no general agreement about what really constitutes Pidgin in Hawai'i. For some people, it means the basilectal variety, with its grammatical rules that are very different from those of English. For others, it means using only the local accent and some local vocabulary items.

In this book, we will concentrate on describing the basilectal or heavy variety of Pidgin—that is, the type Pidgin that is most different from English. But we will mention features of mesolectal or lighter varieties of Pidgin as well.

Chapter 2

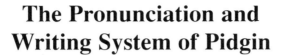

The Pronunciation and Writing System of Pidgin

2.1 The sound system of Pidgin

Pidgin has its own individual system of sounds that are used to distinguish meaning. Consequently, even though most words in Pidgin are derived from English, many are pronounced differently. Here we describe the consonants (usually symbolized by the letters *b, c, d, f, g,* etc.) and the vowels (*a, e, i, o, u*) of Pidgin, concentrating mainly on the differences from English.

2.1.1 The consonant system

As in many other languages, such as French and German, the sound system of basilectal or heavy Pidgin does not include the 'th' sounds, in *thick* and *that*. So in words that come from English, Pidgin speakers may substitute the 't' or 'd' sounds for the 'th' ones—for example, *tink* 'think', *bot* 'both', *dis* 'this', and *fada* 'father'.

On the other hand, the sound system of Pidgin includes some consonants that are not used to distinguish meaning in English. First, there is what linguists call a "flap." In this sound, the tip of the tongue flaps against the ridge behind the upper teeth, as it does when American English speakers pronounce the 't' in *water* in normal speech. Here we'll use a capital 'D' to show this sound. It's found in some Pidgin words of Japanese origin, such as *kaDai* 'spicy hot' and *kaDate* 'karate'. Second, Pidgin includes the glottal stop found in words of Hawaiian origin (as described in section 1.2.2 of Chapter 1), such as *kama'aina* 'person born in Hawai'i or long-term resident' and *Ni'ihau* (an island in the Hawaiian group).

2.1.2 The vowel system

In general American English, there are eleven main vowels, as illustrated by the sounds of the boldfaced letters in the following words:

feet		food
fit		foot
fence	sofa	foam
fat	fun	fall
	father	

English also has a set of sounds (called "diphthongs") made up of two vowels. They are illustrated by the sounds of the boldfaced letters in the following words:

file		fold
fail		foil
	foul	

Heavy Pidgin has the same set of diphthongs, but in contrast to English, it has only seven main vowels, as illustrated below:

feet		food
fake		foam
fat	fun/ father	fall

The 'ee' sound in *feet* and the 'i' sound in *fit* in English are pronounced the same in heavy Pidgin, close to the 'ee' sound in English. So when heavy Pidgin speakers say *hit*, it may sound like *heat* to English speakers.

Similarly, the vowel sounds in *food* and *foot* in English are also pronounced the same in heavy Pidgin, close to the sound of the 'oo' in *boot* in English. So when heavy Pidgin speakers say *look,* it may sound like *Luke*.

In heavy Pidgin, there is an 'e' sound similar to the 'e' sound in Hawaiian or Spanish. It's a bit like the sound of 'a' in *fake* in English, only shorter. But sometimes it sounds almost the same as the 'e' in the English word *bet*.

Also in heavy Pidgin, there's a sound in between the English sounds of 'a' in *fat* and 'e' in *fence*. So the word *bat* might sound like *bet*, and the word *bed* might sound like *bad*. For many heavy Pidgin speakers, *pan* and *pen,* for example, are pronounced the same.

Finally, in heavy Pidgin the sounds of the vowel in *fun* and the first vowel in *father* are pronounced the same, somewhere between the two sounds in English. So the word *bra* and the first syllable of *brother* sound the same, and *pup* may sound like *pop*, or *pop* may sound like *pup*.

The vowel sound of the 'a' in *sofa* in English is not found in most varieties of Pidgin. It is usually replaced by another vowel (see section 2.5.1).

So you can see that the sound system of heavy Pidgin is quite different from that of English, especially with regard to the main vowels. One important thing about Pidgin pronunciation, though, is that there is a lot of variation. The acrolectal, or lighter, varieties (those closer to English) and some mesolectal, or intermediate, varieties have a vowel system almost the same as in general American English. And you can hear some speakers switching back and forth between varieties.

2.2 Writing Pidgin

When you come across Pidgin used in literature, you'll see that the writing system is based on that of English. Sometimes the normal English spelling is used, even though the word is pronounced differently in Pidgin—for example, writing *think* when the word is really pronounced as *tink*. Other times, the spelling is changed to show a different pronunciation, but the rules of English spelling are still used—for example: *tick* 'thick', *kine* 'kind', *odda* 'other', and *respeck* 'respect'. Some writers use an apostrophe to show the absence of a sound or sounds found in the equivalent English word—for example, *t'ink* 'think', *fas'* 'fast', and *j'like* 'just like'.

The problem with English spelling is that some letters can be used for a variety of sounds. For example, compare the different sounds that the letter 'a' represents in these words: *cat, ate, ma, sofa*. Even some of the consonants have different pronunciations, such as 'g' in *game* and *gem*, and 'c' in *cat* and *cell*. Also, some letters in words don't represent any sound at all, such as the 'e' in *make* or the 'a' in *boat*.

But in the writing systems of some languages, such as Hawaiian, each letter (or sometimes a pair of letters) is pronounced, and usually represents only one sound. A similar kind of writing system (or "orthography") was created for Pidgin in the 1970s by Carol Odo, who did a lot of research on the pronunciation of the language (Odo 1975, 1977; Bickerton and Odo 1976). This Pidgin writing system is usually called the "Odo orthography." Although it is used mainly by linguists, on rare occasions it may be found in other contexts, such as in the printed program of the "Wat, Bada yu?" conference held in 1999 on "Hawai'i Creole, Local Identities and Strategies for Multicultural Learning." Also, Lee Tonouchi used the Odo orthography in one short story in his book *Da Word* (2001).

Here are the symbols for vowels used in the Odo orthography. The sound each one represents is the sound of the letter or letters in bold in the English word in the next column. In the next column is that word with Odo spelling. In the last column are other examples of Pidgin words with the symbol, with English spellings in parentheses if they're different.

symbol	sound	Odo spelling	other examples
a	fun or father	*fan/fada*	*ap* (*up*), *mada* (*mother*), *pam* (*palm*)
e	fake	*fek*	*red*, *mek* (*make*), *tude* (*today*)
i	feet	*fit*	*bit* (*beat/bit*), *mi* (*me*), *priti* (*pretty*)
o	foam	*fom*	*brok* (*broke*), *oke* (*okay*), *ol* (*old*)
u	food	*fud*	*but* (*boot*), *gud* (*good*), *yu* (*you*)
ae (or æ)	fat	*faet*	*raep* (*wrap*), *laet* (*let*), *aek* (*act*)
aw	fall	*fawl*	*law*, *awn* (*on*), *tawk* (*talk*)
ai	file	*fail*	*laik* (*like*), *ai* (*I*), *krai* (*cry*)
au	foul	*faul*	*hau* (*how*), *laud* (*loud*), *kau* (*cow*)
ei	fail	*feil*	*eit* (*eight*), *meid* (*maid*), *eij* (*age*)
oi	foil	*foil*	*boil*, *toi* (*toy*), *chois* (*choice*)
ou	fold	*fould*	*vout* (*vote*), *toud* (*toad*), *gout* (*goat*)
r	fur	*fr*	*wrd* (*word*), *hr* (*her*), *bird* (*brd*)

Note that the last symbol is actually for the combination of a vowel plus the 'r' sound that occurs in the middle of words in Pidgin, such as the examples above.

Note also that the symbol 'a' is also sometimes written as 'ɑ', and 'ae' as 'ae'. Also, 'g' may be written as 'ɡ'.

The consonant symbols are mostly the same as in English, but there are a few exceptions. First, the symbol 'zh' is used for the sound of *s* in *measure*. Second, the symbol 'D' is used for the flap in words of Japanese origin, as we mentioned in section 2.1.1. And the *'okina* (') represents the glottal stop, as in Hawaiian.

Another difference is that each of the Odo symbols generally has only one pronunciation. So 'g' is always pronounced as in *game*, never as in *gem*. Also, words are spelled as they sound, not as they look in English. For example, the words *is* and *was* end with an 's' in English, but the sound is really the 'z' sound. So in Odo orthography, they are *iz* and *waz*.

Here is a list of the Odo consonant symbols and some examples (with alternative English spellings, if they exist, in parentheses):

symbol	examples
b	*bawl* (*ball*), *rib*
d	*dawg* (*dog*), *baed* (*bad*)
f	*fani* (*funny*), *inaf* (*enough*)
g	*go*, *baeg* (*bag*)
h	*haed* (*had*), *hou* (*how*)
j	*jank* (*junk*), *baej* (*badge*)
k	*kil* (*kill*), *kik* (*kick*)
l	*ple* (*play*), *pul* (*pull*)
m	*mai* (*my*), *him*
n	*nais* (*nice*), *pin*
p	*pau* 'finished', *grup* (*group*)
r	*raet* (*rat*), *krai* (*cry*)
s	*sel* (*sell*), *mas* (*mus'*, *must*)
t	*tel* (*tell*), *fait* (*fight*)
v	*vaen* (*van*), *neva* (*never*)
w	*wid* (*weed*), *wea* (*where*)
y	*yu* (*you*), *yelo* (*yellow*)
z	*zu* (*zoo*), *izi* (*easy*)
ch	*chek* (*check*), *kaech* (*catch*)
sh	*shel* (*shell*), *fish*
zh	*mezha* (*measure*), *yuzholi* (*usually*)
D	*kaDai* 'spicy hot', *kaDate* (*karate*)
'	*ali'i* 'chief', *Hawai'i*

You may have noticed that there is no 'c', 'q' or 'x' in the Odo orthography. What is spelled as 'c' in English, is either 'k' or 's' in Odo, depending on its sound—for example, *kaet* (*cat*) and *sel* (*cell*). English words with 'q' and 'x' are also spelled as they sound using other symbols—for example, *kwik* (*quick*) and *seks* (*sex*).

The Odo orthography may look a bit strange at first, but once you get used to it, you'll find it's easier than you'd think! We'll use it for the rest of the book, but show English or English-based spelling as well in parentheses.

2.3 Other pronunciation differences between Pidgin and English

2.3.1 't', 'd', and 's' before 'r'

The 't' sound is usually pronounced as 'ch' before 'r', as in *chri* (*tree*) and *chrai* (*try*). The 'd' sound is pronounced as 'j' before 'r', as in *jril* (*drill*) and *jraiv* (*drive*). Also, especially in fast speech, the 's' sound is pronounced as 'sh' before 'r' or 'tr', as in *groshri* (*grocery*) and *shchrit* (*street*).

2.3.2 'r' after vowels

Like the English of New England, Australia, and parts of Britain, the 'r' sound usually does not occur after vowels in heavy Pidgin. So, what is pronounced as *are* in general American English is 'a' in Pidgin—for example: *had* (*hard*) and *paking* (*parking*); *air* is pronounced as 'e' (as in *red*) when preceding another sound—for example, *sked* (*scared*). Also, *or* is pronounced as 'aw' in a stressed (accented) syllable—as in *fawchun* (*fortune*)—but as 'o' in an unstressed (unaccented) syllable, as in *pochrei* (*portray*). (For an explanation of stress, see section 2.5.1.) The exceptions are the words *fo* and *mo*, derived from 'for' and 'more'.

In place of the 'r' at the end of words in English, Pidgin (especially in heavy Pidgin) has a separate syllable 'a', following the sounds represented in Odo by 'i', 'u', 'o', 'ai' or 'e'. Examples are : *dia* (*deer*), *pua* (*poor*), *stoa* (*store*), *faia* (*fire*), and *waelfea* (*welfare*).

As mentioned earlier, the sound of *er* in *her, ir* in *bird, or* in *word*, and *ur* in *burn*, is found in Pidgin, and symbolized as 'r'—for example, *hr, brd, wrd,* and *brn*. But this sound occurs only in separate words such as these, or in stressed syllables, such as in *ritrn* (*return*). In unstressed syllables, in place of this sound in English words, Pidgin has 'e' when followed by another sound—for example, *Rabet* (*Robert*) and *reked* (*record*) [as in 'world record']—and 'a' at the end of a word—for example, *pepa* (*paper*) and *joka* (*joker*).

2.3.3 Syllabic 'l' and 'l' before another consonant

In some English words, the 'l' sound acts as the final syllable by itself—for example *little*. In Pidgin, this 'l' is often replaced by 'o' or 'ol'—for example: *pipo* (*people*), *aepo* (*apple*), *taerabol* (*terrible*). When 'l' precedes another consonant, it may also become 'o' or 'u'—for example, *meok* (*milk*) and *haeup* (*help*). In some words there is variation, such as *rio/riu/ril* (*real*).

2.4 Combinations of sounds

Languages differ in the combinations of sounds they allow. English allows several consonant sounds to be combined into what are called "consonant clusters." For example, the word *strengths* has a cluster of three consonant sounds at the beginning (*s, t, r*) and three at the end (*ng, th, s*). In contrast, some languages, such Hawaiian, do not allow consonant clusters at all. Pidgin has many consonant clusters, but some do not occur at the ends of words.

Where the clusters spelled *pt, ct, ft, st, ld,* and *nd* are found at the end of a word in English, the final sound ('t' or 'd') is absent in basilectal Pidgin—for example: *kep* (*kept*), *aek* (*act*), *sawf* (*soft*), *laes* (*last*), *kol* (*cold*), *spen* (*spend*). Also, in the clusters spelled *ts, ks,* and *ds* at the end of words in English, the sound before the *s* may be absent in Pidgin—for example, *was* (*what's*), *fos* (*folks*), and *kiz* (*kids*).

Also, where the clusters *fr* and *pr* occur in English, the 'r' sound is absent in Pidgin if there is an 'r' at the beginning of the next syllable—for example: *pograem* (*program*), *fashchreited* (*frustrated*), *laibaeri* (*library*).

2.5 Prosodic features

The prosodic features of a language include stress (which syllables are emphasized or accented in a word), speech rhythm, pitch (how high or low speakers' voices go), register (voice quality), and intonation (the way speakers' voices go up or down in different kinds of sentences). (For an early study of the prosodic features of Pidgin, see Vanderslice and Pierson 1967.)

2.5.1 Stress

A stressed syllable in a word is prominent because of a combination of loudness, pitch and length. The meaning of some English words depends on stress. For example, look at these two sentences with the word *present*. (The stressed syllable is shown in bold.)

> He was not **pre**sent for the meeting.
> The principal will pre**sent** the prizes.

In words of three or more syllables, two syllables may be given stress. The stronger stress is called "primary stress," and the weaker "secondary stress." For example, in the word *telepathic, -path-* has primary stress and *tel-* has secondary stress.

In Pidgin, most two-syllable words derived from English have stress on the same syllable as in English. However, there are some exceptions—for example (with the stressed syllable in Pidgin and in the English equivalent both shown in bold): *beis**bawl*** (***base**ball*), *chap**stik*** (***chop**stick*), *he**deik*** (***head**ache*), *ded**lain*** (***dead**line*).

Of words that have more than two syllables, there are many words in Pidgin that have primary stress on a different syllable from that in English. This is especially true of English words in which the first syllable is stressed, such as words ending in *-ary, -ory,* or *-ony*—for example: *diksha**naeri*** (***dic**tionary*), *inven**tawri*** (***in**ventory*), *sera**moni*** (***cer**emony*). Other examples where English and Pidgin stress differ are *hara**kein*** (***hur**ricane*), *aelka**hawl*** (***al**cohol*), *shchraw**bæri*** (***straw**berry*), *haspi**tol*** (***hos**pital*), and *kaeta**lawg*** (***cat**alog*).

Another way in which Pidgin differs from English, at least in the basilectal and sometimes mesolectal varieties, is that syllables that do not have primary stress receive slightly more stress than in English. So a syllable that has no stress in English may have secondary stress in Pidgin. For example, the second syllable in *bebe* (*baby*) and *bilding* (*building*) are emphasized slightly more than in English.

In normal speech in English, the vowel in an unstressed syllable is often not given its full pronunciation. Instead, it is pronounced as the sound of the *a* in ***about*** rather than the way it would be pronounced if it were in a stressed syllable. For example, compare the pronunciations of the underlined vowel in ***org<u>a</u>n*** and ***org<u>a</u>nic***. But because unstressed vowels in English are given more stress in Pidgin, the full vowel is pronounced in many Pidgin words where it is not in English—for example: *kiten* (*kitten*), *wumaen* (*woman*), *Jaepaeniz* (*Japanese*).

2.5.2 Speech rhythm

The combination of full vowels (rather than the sound of the *a* in ***about***) and more stress in what are unstressed syllables in English means that syllables in Pidgin tend to have more equal prominence in terms of loudness and duration than syllables in English. There is also greater stress than in English on function words, such as articles, prepositions, modals, and preverbal tense and aspect markers. (These terms are defined in the following chapter.) Therefore, Pidgin is usually classified as being closer to a "syllable-timed" language like French than to a "stress-timed" language like English.

Syllable-timed means that all syllables tend to occur at approximately equal intervals of time—for example, the sentence *Jawn wen finish hiz homwrk* (*John wen finish his homework*) would be spoken something like this:

Jawn / *wen* / *fin* / *ish* / *hiz* / *hom* / *wrk.*
　1　　　2　　3　　4　　5　　6　　　7

On the other hand, stress-timed means that stressed syllables occur at approximately equal intervals of time—for example:

John has / **fin**ished his / **home**work.
　1　　　　　　2　　　　　　　3

However, syllables or words in Pidgin may be extended or drawled for emphasis, as in this example:

E, yu wen go si da gem yestade? Waz ri::l gu:::d, bra!
(*Eh, you wen go see da game yesterday? Was re::al goo:::d, brah!*)
'Hey, did you go see the game yesterday? It was really really good!'

2.5.3 Pitch and register

In Pidgin, the characteristic range of pitch (how high or low speakers' voices go) is wider than in English, mainly because many Pidgin speakers often use a pitch higher than that found in English.

With regard to voice quality, there are two different registers that are common features of the language. First is the use of raspy voice in drawled syllables or words (mentioned above) or in short periods of extended speech. This functions as a kind of intensifier (to emphasize something) or as a marker of heavy Pidgin, and is used more commonly by men than women. Second is the use of the upper levels of the range of pitch that some researchers have said is a marker of female speech.

2.5.4 Intonation

Intonation refers to the change of pitch through a sentence. One of the most striking differences between Pidgin and English is in the intonation of yes-no questions—that is, questions that can be answered by 'yes' or 'no' (see section 5.8.1). In most varieties of American English, for example, the pattern is rising, starting with intermediate pitch and finishing with high pitch. But in Pidgin, the pattern is falling, starting with high pitch and dropping to low pitch in the last syllable. This is shown in the following examples, where '3' before a group of words, word, or syllable indicates high pitch, '2' intermediate pitch, and '1' low pitch:

Pidgin: ^{3}E, yu wan laif ^{1}gad?

English: ^{2}Are you a ^{3}lifeguard?

Questions ending with the tags *ye* (*yeah*), *e* (*eh*), and *no* (*no*) are very common in Pidgin, and these usually have high pitch. Another tag is also used: *o wat* (or what). This is added to the end of a statement without pausing, and given low pitch and stress:

^{2}*Yu laik go* ^{3}*Maui* ^{1}*o wat?*

'Do you want to go to Maui or what?'

Chapter 3

Word Classes

This is the first chapter about the patterns of words (or grammar) of Pidgin. We will continue the practice of giving Pidgin words in the Odo orthography followed in parentheses by other spellings based on English. But here we'll start using some longer examples as well. Some of these are our own examples, and are given in the Odo orthography. Others are taken from a few works of published literature and from the Pidgin translation of the Bible (*Da Jesus Book*). These examples are given in their original orthography (as they are published), followed by the source (author, year, and page number for literature, and DJB, page number, and biblical reference for examples from *Da Jesus Book*). The full references can be found at the end of this book. The reason for using these examples is so that interested readers can find them in the original work and see them in their larger context.

So, now let's start with Pidgin grammar.

Every language has groups of words that behave in the same way when they are combined with other words to make a sentence. These are called word classes. The specific kinds of word classes and their actual membership may differ from language to language. Pidgin has some classes that are the same as those of English and some that are different.

3.1 Nouns

Nouns are usually words for persons, places, things or ideas, such as *boi* (*boy*), *wahine* 'girl, woman', *maunten* (*mountain*), *haus* (*house*), *flaua* (*flower*), *law*, and *kuleana* 'responsibility'. These examples are of "common nouns." There are also so-called "proper nouns"—names of particular people or places, such as *Lisa* and *Honolulu*.

The class of nouns is also defined by what other kinds of words they can go with. For example, common nouns can occur on their own preceded by *da* (*the*) or *dis* (*this*)—for example, *da boi* (*the boy*) and *dis law* (*this law*).

Some nouns in Pidgin are made up of two words—such as the following examples in which the second word, *gai* (*guy*), is used to indicate a person who does a particular job: *fama gai* (*farmer guy*) 'farmer', *fisha guy* 'fisherman', *ami gai* (*army guy*) 'soldier'.

In English, words that refer to more than one of something are normally marked with the ending *-s* or *-es*, as in *books, cars, houses, churches*, etc. (called the "plural" form). The *-s* is actually sometimes pronounced as 's' as in *cats* and sometimes as 'z' as in *guys*, and the *-es* is pronounced something like 'iz'. In Pidgin, this plural ending is optional. Some speakers use it all the time and others hardly at all. So you might hear *tu pig* (*two pig*) or *tu pigz* (*two pigs*). It's most common when a word ends in a vowel, such as *mai toiz* (*my toys*), and least common when a word is preceded by another word that shows quantity, as in *tu dala* (*two dollar*).

There are also many words in Pidgin that might end in *-s* where it is not found in English—for example: *junks, mails, furnitures, baggages, underwears, slangs, stuffs, corns* 'corn cobs'.

3.2 Pronouns

Pronouns are words that can be used in place of a noun in a sentence, like *he, she*, or *them* in English. Pronouns are often classified according to the "person" they refer to. The "first person" pronoun *I* is used by the speaker to refer to himself or herself; the "second person" pronoun *you* is used by the speaker to refer to the person he or she is talking to, and the "third person" pronoun *he* or *she* (or *it*) is used to refer to another person (or thing) being talked about. English also has the plural forms: first person *we* and third person *they*. (The second person *you* is used for both singular and plural.) These forms of the pronoun are normally used only for the subject of a sentence (the person who is doing the action or being described). Other forms (the object forms) are used in other parts of the sentence—after a verb (section 3.7) or after a preposition (section 3.11): *me, him, her, them*. In English there are also two kinds of "possessive pronouns": describing possessive: *my, your, his, her, its, our, their*, and independent possessive: *mine, yours, his, hers, theirs*. The Pidgin pronouns are given in Tables 1 and 2:

Table 1: Pidgin regular pronouns:

	subject	object
1st person singular	*Ai* (*I*)	*mi* (*me*)
2nd person singular	*yu* (*you*)	*yu* (*you*)
3rd person singular	*hi* (*he*), *shi* (*she*) *him, hr* (*her*),	*him, hr* (*her*) *om* (*em, um*)
1st person plural	*wi* (*we*), *as gaiz* (*us guys*)	*as gaiz* (*us guys*)
2nd person plural	*yu* (*you*), *yu gaiz* (*you guys*)	*yu* (*you*), *yu gaiz* (*you guys*)
3rd person plural	*de* (*dey, they*), *dem gaiz* (*dem guys*)	*dem gaiz* (*dem guys*), *om* (*em*)

Table 2: Pidgin possessive pronouns:

	describing	independent
1st person singular	*ma, mai* (*my*)	*mainz* (*mines*)
2nd person singular	*yoa, yo* (*your*)	*yawz* (*yours*)
3rd person singular	*hiz* (*his*), *hr* (*her*)	*hiz* (*his*), *hrz* (*hers*)
1st person plural	*awa* (*our*)	*awaz* (*ours*)
2nd person plural	*yoa/yo* (*your*), *yu gaiz* (*you guys*)	*yawz* (*yourz*), *yu gaiz* (*you guys*)
3rd person plural	*dea* (*their*)	*deaz* (*theirs*)

Sometimes you'll also hear independent possessive pronouns using *wan* (*one*): *main wan* (*mine one*), *mainz wan* (*mines one*), *yawz wan* (*yours one*), *awaz wan* (*ours one*), *yu gaiz wan* (*you guys one*), *dem gaiz wan* (*them guys one*).

As you can see, most of the Pidgin pronouns are similar to those of English, but there are some important differences. First, Pidgin pronouns most often show plural by adding *gaiz* (*guys*). Second, *it* is rarely used, except in set expressions, like *Stapit!* (*Stop it!*) Rather, other words, such as *da ting* (*the thing*) or *da kain* (*da kine*) (see below) are used instead of *it*, or another Pidgin pronoun *om* (*em, um*) is used after a verb (section 3.7). Third, there's a difference in the form of some of the possessive pronouns, such as *mainz* (*mines*) for 'mine' and *yo* or *yoa* for 'your'.

Fourth, sometimes object pronouns appear at the beginning of the sentence, as in *hr sik* (*her sick*) 'she's sick' and *as go* (*us go*) 'let's go'. Also, object pronouns are used consistently in some places where English uses subject pronouns, for example: *hu him?* (*who him?*) 'who is he?' and *huz san him?* (*whose son him*) 'whose son is he?'.

Finally, unlike English, Pidgin sometimes uses the pronouns *hi* (*he*) and *shi* (*she*) to refer to inanimate objects where *it* is required in English:

*Da stoa **hi** open nain oklak.*
'The store, it opens at nine o'clock.'

*Da klaes **shi** nat daet izi.*
'The class, it isn't that easy.'

*Awl dess tym da saan **he** shynin da wayv **he** braykin . . .*
(bradajo 1998b:171)
(*All this time, the sun, he shining, the wave, **he** breaking . . .*)
'All this time, the sun, it's shining, the wave, it's breaking.'

There's also the other kind of pronoun that has *-self* on the end, called the "reflexive pronoun." The reflexive pronouns in Pidgin are shown in Table 3.

Table 3: Pidgin reflexive pronouns

1st person singular	*maiself (myself)*
2nd person singular	*yoself/yuself (yourself)*
3rd person singular	*himself, hrself (herself)*
1st person plural	*awaself (ourself)*
2nd person plural	*yoself/yuself (yourself)*
3rd person plural	*demself (themself)*

You might also hear: *yuselfs (yourselfs), as gaiz self (us guys self), yu gaiz self (you guys self), dem gaiz self (them guys self)*, and even *demselfs*.

3.3 Determiners

Another word class in Pidgin is made up of words that can precede a noun. This class is called "determiners." As in English, there are two types of determiners.

3.3.1 Articles

Determiners of the first type are called "articles." In English, articles are the small words *the* and *a* (or *an*). The most important articles in Pidgin correspond to these: *da* (*the*) and *wan* (*one*). (Most speakers also use *a* as well, especially in set expressions, such as *a lot* or *wait a while*.)

In English, a distinction is made between definite nouns, preceded by the definite article *the* (such as *the dog*) and indefinite nouns, preceded by the indefinite article *a* (or *an*) (such as *a dog*). Compare these two sentences: *I want to buy the dog* and *I want to buy a dog*. The first one has to refer to a definite dog (one that both the speaker and hearer know about). But the second one may refer to any dog or to one that the speaker knows about, but not the hearer. The same distinction is found in Pidgin:

Ai laik bai da dawg. 'I want to buy the dog.'

Ai laik bai wan dawg. 'I want to buy a dog.'

But there are some differences between the use of articles in English and Pidgin. In English, there are three ways to talk about a person, animal or thing in general (called a "generic" expression)—for example:

The mongoose is smart.

A mongoose is smart.

Mongooses are smart.

Thus, in English, generic expressions can use either the definite or indefinite article with the singular form of the noun, or no article with the plural form of the noun. In Pidgin, however, generic expressions can use either the definite article or (more commonly) no article, both with the singular form of the noun—for example:

Da mangus smat. (*The mongoose smart.*)

Smat da mangus. (*Smart the mongoose.*)

Mangus smat. (*Mongoose smart.*)

So you'll often hear nouns used without an article or plural form, as in

Dawg loyal, not laik kaet. 'Dogs are loyal, not like cats.'

English also uses nouns (in the plural form) without an article when no particular person, place, or thing is being referred to (the "nonspecific" usage)—for example: *He collects coins.* Pidgin uses nouns without an article for the same function, but in the singular form. So, for example:

> *Jawn gon bai buk.*
> 'John's going to buy books.' (he has no particular book in mind)

Compare this with the following, when a specific thing is being referred to:

> *Jawn gon bai da buk.*
> 'John's going to buy the book.' (a particular book that you already know about)
>
> *Jawn gon bai wan buk.*
> 'John's going to buy a book.' (a particular book but one you don't know about)

The similarities and differences between Pidgin and English with regard to the use of articles are summarized in Table 4. (Note that the asterisk [*] means that the following sentence is not acceptable in the language. So, the article *wan* is not normally used for generic sentences in Pidgin.)

Table 4: Articles in Pidgin and English

	Pidgin	**English**
Generic	*Da dawg loyal.*	*The dog is loyal.*
	Dawg loyal.	*Dogs are loyal.*
	*[*Wan dawg loyal.]*	*A dog is loyal.*
Nonspecific	*Ai gon bai wan dawg.*	*I'm gonna buy a dog.*
	Ai gonna bai dawg.	*I'm gonna buy dogs.*
Specific		
hearer doesn't know about it:	*Ai gon bai wan dawg.*	*I'm gonna buy a dog.*
hearer knows about it:	*Ai gon bai da dawg.*	*I'm gonna buy the dog.*

3.3.2 Demonstratives

Determiners of the second type are called "demonstratives." Like English, Pidgin has four of these:

dis (*this, diss*)   *daet* (*that, dat*)

diz (*these, dese*)   *doz* (*those, dose*)

(Sometimes *diskain* and *daetkain* are also used as demonstratives. See section 3.15.)

In English, demonstratives can also be used as pronouns, taking the place of a noun rather than preceding a noun, as in *This is the place* or *That is mine*. The same is true for the Pidgin demonstrative *dis*, as in *Dis da ples* 'This is the place'. But *daet* may become *daes* (*das*) or *aes* (*as*) when it occurs in a sentence without a following noun, as in *Daes mai buk* 'That's my book' and *Aes da gai* 'That's the guy'.

3.4 Quantifiers

Quantifiers are words that refer to the quantity of something. Some Pidgin quantifiers are similar to those of English: *maeni* (*many*) and *sam* (*some*). Different from English is *litobit* or *liDobit* (*little bit*) meaning 'a little bit of', as in *litobit sushi* 'a little bit of sushi'. More common is *pleni* (*plenny*) based on English *plenty* but used in the same way as 'a lot of', as in *pleni pipo* (*plenny peopo*) 'a lot of people' and *pleni rais* 'a lot of rice'. Also, in Pidgin, *tumach* (*too much*) may also be used for 'too many', as in *tumach turis* 'too many tourists'. Other quantifiers are unique to Pidgin: *chok* (*choke*) 'very many' and *uku* 'very many', *uku pleni* 'very very many', and *uku milyan* (*uku million*) 'millions of'.

Cardinal numbers are also quantifiers and are similar to those in English—for example, *tu* (*two*), *nain* (*nine*), *trtin* (*tirteen, thirteen*), *eitifaiv* (*eighty-five*), etc. Ordinal numbers (like *second* and *fourth* in English) are sometimes formed by putting *namba* (*number*) before the cardinal number, as in *namba tu boi* (*number two boy*) 'second son'.

3.5 Adjectives

Adjectives are words used to describe something or someone. Some adjectives in Pidgin are *kyut* (*cute*), *haepi* (*happy*), *kwik* (*quick*), *akamai* 'smart', and *hemajang* 'all mixed up'.

Some words that are nouns can also be used as adjectives. For example, *haole* can be a noun referring to a Caucasian person or an adjective describing someone who looks or acts like a Caucasian; *jank* (*junk*) can refer to junk or it can be used to describe something that isn't good.

3.6 Degree modifiers

To show the comparative (*bigger, taller,* etc.), the word *mo* is put before the adjective—for example: *mo big* 'bigger', *mo skini* 'skinnier'. The exceptions are saying it's *mo baeta* (*mo betta*), and *mo wrs* (*mo worse*) instead of **mo gud* (*mo good*) or **mo baed* (*mo bad*).

(Remember, an asterisk [*] before a group of words means that this is not an acceptable way of saying something. In other words, you wouldn't normally hear anyone saying something like that.)

The phrase *mo litobet* means 'less' or 'fewer,' as in *Hau kam ai get mo litobit daen yu?* 'How come I have less (or fewer) than you?'.

The word *mo* belongs to a class of words that can come before adjectives, quantifiers, and adverbs (see below) called "degree modifiers." Examples of *mo* used before quantifiers are *mo pleni* (*more plenty*) 'more' and *mo litobit* (*more little bit*) 'less'.

Sometimes you might hear people using a combination of the Pidgin system and the English system, as in *mo tawla* (*more taller*).

Other degree modifiers include *tu* (*too*), *so,* and *ril* (*real*) as in *tu gud* (*too good*), *so haole,* or *ril hangri* (*real hungry*). One difference from English is that *sam* (*some*) is also used as a degree modifier, as in *dea haus sam smawl* (*their house some small*) 'their house is really small'. Note that the English word *very* is not commonly used in heavy Pidgin.

Another degree modifier is *kinda* (*kind of*), which means 'a bit' or 'somewhat', as in *kinda big*. (This may be due to the influence of English.)

3.7 Verbs

Verbs are most often words that refer to an action or something happening—for example: *ran* (*run*), *it* (*eat*), *stadi* (*study*), and *mek* (*make*). These are called "active verbs." But another type of verb refers to a relatively permanent condition or state—for example: *no* (*know*), *get* 'have', *laik* (*like*), and *fil* (*feel*). These are called "stative verbs" (section 4.5.1).

Verbs in Pidgin generally have only two forms: the plain form—such as *go, teik* (*take*), *wawk* (*walk*), and *it* (*eat*)—and a form with *-ing* attached—such as *teiking* (*taking*), *wawking* (*walking*), and *iting* (*eating*). As in English, the *-ing* form of the verb is used to indicate an ongoing or continuing action. Also, as in English, the *-ing* ending is sometimes pronounced as *-in*.

Many verbs in Pidgin, as in English, are made up of two words. These are called "phrasal verbs." The most common phrasal verbs include words such as *awn* (*on*), *aet* (*at*), *ap* (*up*), *aut* (*out*), and *awf* (*off*)—for example: *put awn* (*put on*), *luk aet* (*look at*), *bit ap* (*beat up*), *weik ap* (*wake up*), *fain aut* (*find out*), *chrou aut* (*throw out*), and *teik awf* (*take off*). Most have meanings the same as in English.

3.8 Tense markers

Tense refers to the time when the action or state of a verb occurs—such as past or future. In English there are different ways of showing tense:

(1) a separate word is used before the verb, as with *will* used to show future tense: *They will work tomorrow.*
(2) the form of the verb is changed: for example, *take* becomes *took* for past tense; other pairs include *sing/sang, write/wrote, eat/ate.*
(3) a suffix is added onto the verb, as with *-ed* used to show past tense: *They worked yesterday.*

Pidgin uses mainly the first way of showing tense—that is, a separate word before the verb. These words are called "tense markers," and there are three different kinds: the future marker, the past tense marker, and the past habitual marker.

3.8.1 Future marker

Future events and states and those that have not yet occurred are marked by *gon* (*goin, going*), similar in some ways to English *am/is/are/was/were going to* or *gonna*:

Ai **gon** bai wan pikap.
'I'm going to buy a pickup.'

*She **goin** miss da prom.* (Kearns 2000:13)
'She'll miss the prom.'

Future events (but not states) can also be indicated by the verb *go* occurring directly before an active verb (section 4.5.2.5).

3.8.2 *Past marker*

Past tense is often not marked in Pidgin (see section 4.5.4), but when it is, it is most often indicated by *wen* before the verb:

*Dass 'cause dey **wen'** paint his skin.* (Morales 1988:72)
'That's because they painted his skin.'

*Ai **wen** si om.*
'I saw him.'

In rapid speech, *wen* is sometimes reduced to *en* or just *n* as in the following example:

*Make me feel like da bugga in da play we'**n** read lass year.*
(Kearns 2000:5)
'He makes me feel like the guy in the play we read last year.'

Two other words are also used by some people to mark past tense: *bin,* especially by speakers of heavy pidgin and older speakers, and *haed* (*had*), especially by speakers from the island of Kaua'i:

*Ai **bin** klin ap mai ples fo da halade.*
'I cleaned up my place for the holidays.'

*De **haed** plei BYU laes wik.*
'They played BYU last week.'

3.8.3 *Past habitual marker*

The marker *yustu* (*use to*) occurs before the verb to indicate habitual or frequent actions or states from the past, or past habitual:

*Ai **yustu** plei futbawl.*
'I used to play football.'

*Your mahda **use to** tink so.* (Kearns 2000:10)
'Your mother used to think so.'

Some older speakers have combined Pidgin and English by using Pidgin *yustu* to mark past habitual and following it with the English infinitive construction (e.g., *to go*)—for instance:

*Ai **yustu tu** tink so.*
'I used to think so.'

3.9 Modals

Another class of words that occur before verbs are the "modals." These are words that express things like ability, permission, obligation, and possibility. In English, the modals are words such as *can, should, must,* and *have to*. In Pidgin, the modals are as follows:

kaen (can) indicates permission, ability or possibility:

*Jo mada tel him hi no **kaen** go.*
'Joe's mother told him he couldn't go.'

*You tink you **can** lift dis?* (Lum 1999:23)
'Do you think you can lift this?'

laik (like) indicates volition or wanting to do something:

*Ai **laik** go Vegas.*
'I want to go to Las Vegas.'

*You **like** come?* (Ching 1998:182)
'Do you want to come?'

Note that in English, *want* acts as a verb, but the equivalent in Pidgin, *laik* (*like*), acts as a modal (occurring directly before the plain form of a verb). But sometimes *laik* (*like*) does act as a verb in Pidgin—when it means 'like' and occurs before a noun or the *-ing* form of a verb, as in

> *Mama rili **laik** daet wan.*
> 'Mama really likes that one.'

> *Ai **laik** going Las Vegas.*
> 'I like going to Las Vegas.'

Other modals indicate various degrees of obligation.

gata (***gotta***) implies some outside pressure to do something now or in the future:

> *Ai **gata** bring om maiself.*
> 'I've got to bring it myself.'

> *Okay, but I **gotta** eat early.* (Tonouchi 1998:245)
> 'Okay, but I have to eat early.'

haeftu (***have to***) also implies a necessity to do something:

> *Jo **haeftu** wrk frs bifo hi kaen plei.*
> 'Joe has to work first before he can play.'

> *All da time you **have to** try your best.* (Lum 1998b:227)
> 'You always have to try your best.'

baeta (***bettah, better***) indicates that it would be good to do something or else something bad might happen:

> *You **bettah** quit that, or we going broke yo' head!* (Pak 1998a:117)
> 'You'd better quit that or we'll break your head!'

> *So, you **betta** do um!* (DJB:14 [Matt.5:33])
> 'So, you'd better do it!'

sapostu (*suppose to*) can imply a past obligation as well as a present or future one:

> *Bil **sapostu** finish hiz homwrk yestadei bat hi neva finish.*
> 'Bill was supposed to finish his homework yesterday, but he didn't finish it.'

> *You **suppose to** call da teachas at UH "doctah"* . . . (Kearns 2000:27)
> 'You're supposed to call the teachers at UH "doctor" . . . '

3.10 Adverbs

Adverbs are words that describe when (time), where (place), or how (direction or manner) the action or state of a verb or adjective occurs. Adverbs of time include *yestadei* (*yesterday*), *nau* (*now*), *leita* (*later*, *lata*), *samtaimz* (*sometimes*), names of days of the week, and expressions such as *las yia* (*last year*). Some adverbs of time in Pidgin that differ from English are *aefta* (*after*) meaning 'afterwards', *evritaim* (*every time*) meaning 'all the time, always', and *sem taim* (*same time*) or *da sem taim* meaning 'at the same time':

> *Learning Latin da hard part. Everyting else duck soup **afta**.*
> (Kearns 2000:34)
> 'Learning Latin is the hard part. Everything else is easy afterwards.'

> *My small sista **everytime** get lickens.* (Yamanaka 1998b:156)
> 'My little sister always gets a beating.'

> *Ai dono hau hi kaen tawk aen it **sem taim**.*
> 'I don't know how he can talk and eat at the same time.'

(Note that time expressions such as *yestadei* (*yesterday*), *tumaro* (*tomorrow*), days of the week, etc., can also be used as nouns. Others, such as *bifo* and *aefta*, can be used as prepositions [section 3.11].)

Another common adverb of time is *bambai* (*bumbye*, *by'm'by*), which can mean 'later, eventually, finally, after a while', etc.—for example:

Bumbye, *da odda girls wen come.* (DJB:77 [Matt.25:11])
'After a while, the other girls came.'

He wen stot cracking up, **bumbye** *he wen cough so hard he gotta go turn on da ventilator.* (Kearns 2000:22).
'He started cracking up. Eventually, he coughed so hard he had to turn on the ventilator.'

This word has another function as a connector (section 6.4).

One of the most frequent adverbs in Pidgin is *awredi* or *awrede* (*already*, *awready*). It sometimes means the same as English *already*, but it is also used with a slightly different meaning, indicating that an action or a state is complete or has already come to pass. When used in this way, the word usually comes at the end of the phrase or sentence:

You wen fail **already**. (Kearns 2000:11)
'You already failed.'

Dah buggah dead **already**. (Pak 1998b:321)
'The poor guy's dead.'

I'm old **already**. (Lum 1998b:226)
'I'm (already) old.'

Also, *awredi* or *awrede* (*already*, *awready*) can be used with negatives where English would use *anymore*:

Da tako no come in **already** *Olowalu-side.* (Masuda 1998:232)
'The octopus doesn't come to the Olowalu area anymore.'

Adverbs of place include *hia* (*here*) and *dea* (*dere*, *there*). Often *ovahia* or *ohia* (*over here*) and *ovadea* or *odea* (*over there*) are used to mean just 'here' and 'there'. In Pidgin, names of particular locations are also used as adverbs of place, like the word *home* is used in English. So as in English where you can say *we come home*, in Pidgin you can say *wi kam Hilo* (*we come Hilo*) 'we come to Hilo'.

Adverbs of direction are words like *ap* (*ap*), *daun* (*down*), and *aut* (*out*). (They can also be used as prepositions [section 3.11].) Pidgin also has two adverbs of direction derived from Hawaiian: *makai* 'toward the sea' and *mauka* 'toward the mountain or inland'.

Adverbs of manner in English are often formed by adding *-ly* to an adjective, for example *quickly* and *slowly*. But some adverbs use the same form as the adjective—for example, *fast*. Some Pidgin adverbs also end in *-li* (*-ly*)—for example, *definitli* (*definitely*), but others only use the same form as the adjective—for example, *kwik* (*quick*) 'quickly' and *slou* (*slow*) 'slowly', as in *De wawk slou* (*they walk slow*).

3.11 Prepositions

Prepositions are those small words that give a location: such as *aet* (*at*), *in*, *awn* (*on*), *ova* (*over*); describe a movement: *tu* (*to*), *fram* (*from*), *chru* (*through*), *ap* (*up*), *daun* (*down*); deal with a tool or accompaniment: *wit* (*with*), or with a beneficiary: *fo* (*for*). They differ from adverbs of direction in that they are always part of a larger group of words (called a prepositional phrase; see section 4.3).

One common Pidgin preposition that is used differently from English is *awntap* (*on top*), which means simply 'on', as in *awntap da teibol* 'on the table'. Also, *insaid* (*inside*) is often used to mean simply 'in'—for example: *insaid da stawri* (*inside the story*) 'in the story'. And *infran* (*in front*) means 'in front of', as in *infrant evribadi* 'in front of everybody'.

3.12 Postmodifiers

Pidgin has a word class not found in English. Words in this class occur after a single word or a group of words and modify or classify the preceding word or group of words in some way. These are called "postmodifiers," and include the following: *taim* (*time*), *said* (*side*), *kain* (*kine, kind*), *gaiz* (*guys*), *foks* (*folks*), and *dem*.

A word or group of words followed by *taim* (*time*) describes a particular time or acts as an adverb of time, telling when something happened. For example, *bifo taim* (*before time*) means 'in the past', and *smawl kid taim* (*small kid time*) means 'when we were little kids'. Also, *taim* is used with demonstratives—for example, *dis taim* (*this time*) 'now' and *daet taim* (*that time*) 'then'.

Similarly, a word or group of words followed by *said* (*side*) describes a particular place or acts as an adverb of place, such as *Mililani said* (*Mililani side*) 'in the area of Mililani' and *dauntaun Hilo said* (*downtown Hilo side*) 'in downtown Hilo'. Again, *said* is also used with demonstratives: *dis said* (*this side*) 'here' and *daet said* (*that side*) 'there'.

In the same way, a word or group of words followed by *kain* (*kine, kind*) acts as an adjective to describe something—for example:

*She put her hand by her mout and make **geisha-kine** giggle, so fake.*
(Lum 1998b:227)

*De wen bai enikain **no nid kain** stafs.*
'They bought many kinds of things they don't need (i.e., unneeded stuff).'

As we have seen with the pronouns, one function of *gaiz* (*guys*) is to show plural, as in *da einjel gaiz* (*da angel guys*) 'the angels' and *yoa aens-esta gaiz* (*your ancestor guys*) 'your ancestors'. But after a noun, it can also mean something like 'and those associated with' that noun—for example:

*She axed me where **my mom guys** went.* (Tonouchi 1998:249)
'She asked me where my mom and those with her went.'

Sometimes *foks* (*folks*) is used in a similar way:

*Last weekend I was suppose to go wit **Vernalani folks** to da Pure Heart concert.* (Kearns 2000:29)

Similarly, *dem* after a noun means 'and other associated people':

***Kaerol dem** wen go shaping yestade.*
'Carol and the others went shopping yesterday.'

*Lata, **Jesus dem** wen go away from Jericho town.*
(DJB:61 [Matt.20:29])
'Later, Jesus and his disciples went away from Jericho.'

3.13 Interjections

Interjections in English are expressions such as *oh, gosh, wow, damn, gee,* etc. (and also some rude ones that we won't include here!). Some common interjections in Pidgin are *o* (*oh*), *ae* or *e* (*eh*), *ho, wo* (*whoa*), *aisus, ai karamba, auwe, ho ka, ho ke,* and *hala.* (The last four are from Hawaiian.) Words from other classes can also be used as interjections—for example: *Kul!, Nat!, Chi!, Shit!, Wot!, Bachi!*

This class of words is most commonly found in a sentence type called "exclamations" (section 5.9).

3.14 Discourse particles

Discourse particles are the small words used to keep a narrative going or get feedback from the listener—for example, *eh, you know,* and *you see* in English. Pidgin has several discourse particles, which are used quite frequently: *ae, yae* (*yeah*), or *e* (*eh*), *ha* (*huh*), and *no.* The use of these discourse particles is described in section 5.10.

3.15 Multifunctional words

As we have seen, a particular word, such as *jank* (*junk*), can be a member of different word classes, depending on how it is used or how it functions in a sentence. The same is true in English, where for example, the word *drink* can be a noun, as in *I need a drink,* or a verb, as in *We drink wine with our dinner.* Words that can be members of more than one word class and that have several functions are said to be "multifunctional."

One of the most multifunctional words in Pidgin is *kain* (*kine, kind*). We have already seen in section 3.12 that it can act as a postmodifier. But it can also function as a noun with the meaning 'kind' or 'kinds'—for example:

> . . . *those pure bred **kine**, dey die young.* (Tonouchi 1998:248)
> ' . . . those pure bred kinds, they die young.'

> *Yu frai da smawl **kain** ril gud, yu kaen it da hol ting.*
> 'If you fry the small kind [of fish] really good, you can eat the whole thing.'

As it does when used as a postmodifier, *kain* can occur before another noun with the meaning 'kind of' as in

*How dah hell we goin' sell dis **kine** produce?* (Pak 1998b:320)
'How the hell are we going to sell this kind of produce?'

*What **kine** glove dis?* (Chock 1998:28)
'What kind of glove is this?'

*. . . we neva see dis **kine** stuff happen befo.* (DJB:27 [Matt.9:33])
' . . . we didn't see this kind of thing happening before.'

Also, *kain* is frequently used with adjectives where *kind of* would not necessarily be used in English, implying that other kinds exist:

*da small **kine** beads* (Lum 1998a:71)
'the small beads'

*All da trees dat no give good **kine** fruit, dey cut um down . . .*
(DJB:20 [Matt.7:19])
'They cut down all the trees that don't give good fruit . . . '

In addition, *kain* (*kine*) is used with adjectives or quantifiers when no nouns follow:

*I know you already done planny **kine** fo help me out lately . . .*
(Kearns 2000:34)
'I know you've already done plenty to help me out lately . . . '

*. . . da gun was funny **kine*** (Lum 1998a:71)
' . . . the gun was funny.'

The word *enikain* (*anykine*) can be used as an adjective meaning 'many kinds of' or as a noun meaning 'anything' or 'everything':

*. . . she had **anykine** good luck cats* (Lum 1998b:224)
' . . . she had many kinds of good luck cats.'

*She know **anykine** so I was worried . . .* (Lum 1998b:228)
'She knows everything so I was worried . . . '

Sometimes, *awl kain* (*all kine*) can be used for 'all kinds of':

*Yoa ancestor guys wen teach **all kine** stuff.* (DJB:45 [Matt.15:3])
'Your ancestors taught all kinds of things.'

Finally, *dakain* (*da kine*) is one of the most versatile expressions in Pidgin, having several uses. First it can mean 'the kind of' or 'that kind of' as in

*Aes **dakain** gaiz ai no laik.*
'That's the kind of guys I don't like.'

Second, it can mean 'of this/that kind, of these/those' as in

*Ai get tu **da kain**.*
'I have two of these.'

Third, it is used when you can't think of a word right away, or when you think the listener might not know the word:

*Wi wen shut sam **da kain**, faesants.*
'We shot some, what do you call them, pheasants.'

*Da Indians had, **da kine**, leather pants wit da fringes.* (Lum 1998a:71)
'The Indians had, what's their name, leather pants with the fringes.'

Fourth, it is used as a substitute for another word. This is like English *whachamacallit* or *doohinky*—when you can't think of the word—or when the person you're talking to will know what you're referring to:

*De yustu haev wan **dakain**.*
'They used to have a whachamacallit.'

But unlike any word in English, *dakain* can replace not only nouns, but words from other classes, including verbs—for example:

*Ai gon **dakain** om.*
'I'm gonna do something to him [you know what I mean].'

It can also be used as a euphemism—a word used in place of a taboo word or something that someone is too embarrassed or forbidden to say— as in

*Lisa saw hiz **dakain**.*
'Lisa saw his "thing."'

*I neva tell you about Florence? You know—about da—**da kine**.*
(Kearns 2000:10)
'Didn't I tell you about Florence? You know—about the—the thing.'

Basically, *dakain* (*da kine*) can be used whenever you know that the person you're talking to will know what you mean. Its use emphasizes a bond of shared experience between people, and in this way epitomizes Pidgin. So when Elizabeth Carr titled her book *Da Kine Talk,* people familiar with the culture of Hawaiʻi knew it was about Pidgin.

Another common multifunctional word in Pidgin is *laidaet* (*lidat, liʻdat*). It can follow the verb or adjective with the meaning 'like that' or 'in that way', as in the following sentence:

*He talking **lidat** cuz we neva bring da food.* (DJB:49 [Matt.16:7])
'He's talking like that because we didn't bring the food.'

*. . . he practice sound all smot **liʻdat**.* (Kearns 2000:20)
'. . . he practiced sounding all smart like that.'

Or it can follow a noun, as in

*I nevah get dress shoes **liʻdat**.* (Tonouchi 1998:248)
'I didn't have dress shoes like that.'

Also, *laidaet* (*lidat, liʻdat*) can be used to mean 'and so on' or 'etcetera' or 'and things like that' or 'something like that', as in

*But Shakespeare like talking about da seasons and ships **li'dat**.* (Kearns 2000:25)

*Wuz Valentine's Day so I went fo' visit her drop off candy **li'dat**.* (Tonouchi 1998:245)

*Hau kam yu ste awl nais **laidaet**?*
'Why are you being so nice and everything?'

3.16 Other word classes

Other word classes are introduced in later sections of this book. These include auxiliaries (section 4.5.2.3), negative markers (5.6), question words (5.8), conjunctions (6.1 and 6.2.1), complementizers (6.2.3), relativizers (6.2.4), and connectors (6.4).

Chapter 4

Phrases

A phrase is a series of words combined to form a part of a sentence. As in most languages, there are five different kinds of phrases in Pidgin: adjective phrase (AdjP), adverb phrase (AdvP), noun phrase (NP), prepositional phrase (PP), and verb phrase (VP). We describe the structure of a phrase according to the word classes that are combined to make it up.

4.1 Adjective phrase (AdjP)

An adjective phrase (AdjP) is made up of an adjective that may be preceded by a degree modifier. An example is: *ril big* 'really big'. Sometimes an AdjP occurs with just an adjective alone—for example, just *big*.

There's a shorthand notation used to describe the structure of phrases. First, we use an arrow to mean 'is made up of the following word classes as components'. Second, if a word class is optional (meaning sometimes it's a component of the phrase and sometimes it's not), then we put it in parentheses. So **AdjP → (degree modifier) adjective** means "an adjective phrase is made up of an adjective and an optional degree modifier."

There's also another kind of AdjP. This is the kind that is made up of a group of words preceding the postmodifier *kain* (*kine*), as described in section 3.12.

4.2 Noun phrase (NP)

A noun phrase (NP) is normally made up of a noun that may be preceded by other word classes or phrases. These include determiners (which can be either the articles *da, wan* (*one*), *a*, or the demonstratives *dis, daet, diz, doz*, quantifiers (including numerals), or an AdjP. Here are some examples of NPs and their components:

fish	'fish'	noun
da fish	'the fish'	determiner[article] noun
doz fish	'those fish'	determiner[demonstrative] noun
chri fish	'three fish'	quantifier noun
doz chri fish	'those three fish'	determiner quantifier noun
ril big fish	'really big fish'	AdjP noun
doz ril big fish	'those really big fish'	determiner AdjP noun
chri ril big fish	'three really big fish'	quantifier AdjP noun
doz chri ril big fish	'those three really big fish'	determiner quantifier AdjP noun

So the shorthand for the structure of a Pidgin NP is:

NP → (determiner) (quantifier) (AdjP) noun.

Of course, this shorthand doesn't work for all NPs. For example, when the noun in an NP is a proper noun (the name of a person or place, like *Carol* or *Maui*), then it generally cannot be preceded by a determiner, quantifier, or AdjP. Also, there are some NPs that include a postmodifier at the end (section 3.12).

A special kind of NP is one that indicates possession, such as *the boy's little puppy* in English. A possessive NP is actually made up of two smaller NPs: one referring to the possessor (such as *the boy*) and the other to the possession (such as *little puppy*). In a possessive NP, the possessor part takes the place of the determiner, and in English it is followed by *'s*. Possessive NPs in Pidgin are similar to those of English, except that the *'s* is not always required. So, you can hear possessive NPs such as: *Jo haus* (*Joe house*) 'Joe's house' and *da wahine nu kar* (*da wahine new car*) 'the woman's new car'.

There is also another type of NP. In this type, a whole NP of the kind we've just been looking at is replaced by a pronoun. So, suppose someone asks

Wea doz chri ril big bots ste? 'Where are those three really big boats?'

The answer could be

De ste Hilo nau. 'They're at Hilo now.'

Here the pronoun *de* 'they' takes the place of the whole NP, not just the noun. (In fact we need to revise the definition of a pronoun that we saw in section 3.2. It should be "A pronoun is a word that can be used in place of a noun phrase.")

An NP that has been replaced by a pronoun has the simple structure **NP → pronoun**.

4.3 Prepositional phrase (PP)

A prepositional phrase (PP) is made up of a preposition followed by a noun phrase—for example: *awn wan smawl ailaen* 'on a small island', *ausaid da haus* 'outside the house', *fo him* 'for him'. So the structure is **PP → P NP**.

A prepositional phrase can occur as part of a noun phrase—for example: *da gai fram Maui* 'the guy from Maui', and *doz chri ril big fish insaid da tenk* 'those three really big fish in the tank'. So, we need to revise the structure of the noun phrase given in section 4.2 to the following:

NP → (determiner) (quantifier) (AdjP) noun (PP)

A PP can also occur as part of another type of phrase, as described in section 4.5 below.

4.4 Adverb phrase (AdvP)

Just as there are four kinds of adverbs (section 3.10), so there are four kinds of adverb phrases (AdvP):

(1)   AdvP of time: words such as *tumaro* (tomorrow), combinations of words such as *neks wik* (*next week*), and groups of words preceding the postmodifier *taim* (*time*), such as *smawl kid taim* (*small kid time*) 'childhood'.

(2)   AdvP of place: words such as *hia* (*here*), names of places such as *Kona* or *meinlaen* (*mainland*), and groups of words preceding the postmodifier *said* (*side*), such as *Waimānalo said* (*side*).

(3)   AdvP of direction: *ap* (*up*), *daet we* (*that way*), *mauka* 'inland'.

(4)   AdvP of manner: sometimes the same as an adjective phrase (AdjP) such as *ril slo* (*real slow*) 'very slowly'.

4.5 Verb phrase (VP)

The verb phrase (VP) can be made up of just a verb, as in the following (the VP is underlined):

Ran! (*Run!*)
Ai no. (*I know.*)
Jim wrk. (*Jim work.*) 'Jim works.'

As mentioned in section 3.7, verbs in Pidgin normally have two forms—the plain form and the form with the *-ing* ending, which indicates a continuing action, as in English. In Pidgin, the *-ing* form of the verb can occur on its own in a VP:

Da kaet iting. (*The cat eating.*)
'The cat is eating.'

Mai brada gaiz sliping. (*My brother guys sleeping.*)
'My brothers are sleeping.'

But most of the time a VP is made up of a main verb with other words. First we'll look at the word classes and phrases that can come after the main verb in a verb phrase, and then at those that can come before the main verb.

4.5.1 Words and phrases that come after the main verb

First of all, the main verb may be followed by a noun or noun phrase (NP), as in the following (the VP is underlined and the NP is in bold):

*Hi plei **beisbawl**.* (*He play **baseball**.*)

*Yu si **da big dawg**?* (*You see **the big dog**?*)

*Mai fada kaeri **om**.* (*My father carry **'em**.*)

Remember, there are two kinds of verbs: stative and active (section 3.7). A limited number of stative verbs may be followed by an adjective or adjective phrase (AdjP). These verbs include *kam* (*come*) (here meaning 'become'), *bi* (*be*), *ste* (*stei, stay*), *luk* (*look*), *fil* (*feel*), and *get*. Here are some examples, with the verb phrase underlined and with the AdjP in bold:

*And den everyting come **quiet**.* (Lum 1999:19)
'And then everything became quiet.'

*. . . I goin be **awesome**!* (DJB:75 [Matt.24:30])
' . . . I'm going to be awesome.'

*. . . you guys no stay **strong inside**.* (DJB:26 [Matt.26:41])
' . . . you are all weak.'

*Make their stomach look **mo skinny**.* (Lum 1999:19)
'It makes their stomach look skinnier.'

*Dey wen feel **real good** inside.* (DJB:3 [Matt.2:10])
'They felt really good inside.'

*She weng get **skwash** . . .* (bradajo 1998a:21)
'She got squashed . . .'

Note that in this context, the Pidgin meanings of two of these verbs are different from their English meanings: *kam* (*come*) means 'become' and *ste* (*stei, stay*) 'am, is, are, was, or were'. When *ste* (*stei, stay*) is used in this way (before an AdjP), it is acting as a "linking verb."

The verb by itself, or with an NP or AdjP after it, may be followed by a prepositional phrase (PP), for example:

*Dey stay standing **on top da beach***. (DJB:38 [Matt.13:2])
'They were standing on the beach.'

*And den everyting come quiet **for one second***. (Lum 1999:21)
'And then everything became quiet for a second.'

*De ple futbawl **in da pak***.
'They play football in the park.'

Finally, an adverb phrase (AdvP) can come after the verb or at the end of the VP.

time: *He going wrestle **next week***. (Lum 1998b:228)
   'He'll wrestle next week.'

place: *As gaiz kaen go pati **yo haus***.
   'We can go party at your house.'

direction: *One guy . . . went come and screw da coffin cover **down***. (Lum 1999:26)
   'A guy came and screwed the coffin cover down.'

manner: *He talk **slow***.
   'He talks slowly.'

In summary, so far with regard to constituents following the main verb, we have seen two kinds of VP:

VP → **V**stative   **(AdjP)**   **(PP)** **(AdvP)**
             or **(NP)**
VP → **V**active   **(NP)**   **(PP)** **(AdvP)**

4.5.2 Words that come before the main verb

4.5.2.1 Tense markers and modals

We'll start with the first word in the VP. This may be either a tense marker or a modal (sections 3.8 and 3.9). Here are some examples of verb phrases beginning with a tense marker:

*She **goin** born one boy.* (DJB:2 [Matt.1:21])
'She's going to give birth to a boy.'

*Damien **going** spock us* . . . (Pak 1998a:111)
'Damien will see us.'

*Charaine Fong **wen** catch food poisoning from one plate lunch.* (Kearns 2000:5)
'Charaine Fong caught food poisoning from a plate lunch.'

*Dey **wen** cut down da mango tree* . . . (Tonouchi 1998:245)
'They cut down the mango tree . . . '

Here are some examples of VPs beginning with modals:

*You **can** tell she smot.* (Kearns 2000:24)
'You can tell she's smart.'

*Okay, but I **gotta** eat early.* (Tonouchi 1998:245)
'Okay, but I have to eat early.'

*All da time you **have to** try your best.* (Lum 1998b:227)
'You always have to try your best.'

*So, you **betta** do um!* (DJB:14 [Matt.5:33])
'You'd better do it!'

Tense markers can occur before the modals *kaen* (*can*), *laik* (*like*), *haeftu* (*have to*), and *sapostu* (*supposed to*), but some of these are quite infrequent:

*Hi **bin kaen** go?*
'Was it possible for him to go?'

*Herod **wen like** kill him*. (DJB:43 [Matt.14:5])
'Herod wanted to kill him.'

*De **gon kaen** kam o wat?*
'Will they be able to come or what?'

*Yu **gon haeftu** pau da wrk*.
'You're going to have to finish the work.'

*Shi **wen sapostu** klin da haus*.
'She was supposed to clean the house.'

4.5.2.2 *chrai* (*try*)

The verb *chrai* (*try*) 'try' can also occur before the main verb and after a tense marker or modal:

*I went **try** draw one horn of plenty* . . . (Lum 1998a:71)
'I tried to draw a horn of plenty . . . '

*I like **try** explain someting to you*. (Kearns 2000:13)
'I want to try and explain something to you.'

As you will see in section 5.7, *chrai* (*try*) also functions as a softener or politeness marker in commands.

4.5.2.3 Auxiliaries

The verbs *ste* (*stei, stay*), *stat* (*start*), and *pau* 'finish' can occur before the main verb as well. In this position, they have the special function of giving some additional information about the action, event, or state of the main verb—for example, about whether it is started or continuing, or whether it is completed. (In grammatical terms, this is called "aspect.") In this function, these verbs are called "auxiliaries." They occur mainly before active verbs such as *ran* (*run*) and *sing*, but can also occur before some stative verbs, such as *kam* (*come*) 'become'.

The most common auxiliary is *ste* (*stei, stay*). This is used to indicate that the action of the verb is continuing (or "progressive" aspect). It can occur before either the plain form of the verb, or more commonly, the *-ing* form:

*Wat yu **ste** it*?
'What are you eating?'

*Wi **ste** mekin da plaen.*
'We're making the plan.'

*. . . my grandpa **stay** listening to his Japanese radio station.*
(Tonouchi 1998:245)
' . . . my grandpa is listening to his Japanese radio station.'

*I **stay** drowning my sorrows in Faye and Shakespeare.*
(Kearns 2000:26)
'I was drowning my sorrows in Faye and Shakespeare.'

For some speakers, the use of *ste* with the *-ing* form of the verb implies an action that is in progress just at the moment, while *ste* with the plain form of the verb implies a longer-lasting or habitual action.

Nowadays in Pidgin, the auxiliary *ste* is frequently left out, and progressive action may be indicated with just the *-ing* form of the verb, as already mentioned:

He helping me. (Ching 1998:187)
'He's helping me.'

She talking to herself. (Lum 1998b:230)
'She's talking to herself.'

I t'ink Chunky playing one big joke on us. (Pak 1998a:116)
'I think Chunky is playing a big joke on us.'

And Chubby Roland he leading da kids like one choochoo train . . .
(Lum 1999:27)
'And Chubby Roland was leading the kids like a choochoo train . . . '

The auxiliary *ste* (*stei, stay*) can also be used to indicate a state or condition that results from the action or state of the verb being accomplished. (This is called "perfective" aspect). In this case, only the plain form of the verb can be used (not the *-ing* form). Here are some examples:

*Ai **ste** kuk da stu awredi.*
'I already cooked the stew.'

*Evribadi **ste finish**.*
'Everyone is finished.'

*When I **stay** come one old man* . . . (Kearns 2000:26)
'When I've become an old man . . . '

The next auxiliary, *stat* (*start*), indicates that the action of the main verb will begin or has begun. (This is called "inchoative" aspect.) It occurs before the *-ing* form of the main verb:

*Mai sista gon **stat** pleing saka.*
'My sister is going to start playing soccer.'

*I wen' **start** eating the Raisinets all one time.* (Yamanaka 1998a:153)
'I started eating the Raisinets all at once.'

The third auxiliary is *pau*, which can also be used as a main verb meaning 'finish' or an adjective meaning 'finished'. As an auxiliary it occurs before the plain form of the main verb and indicates that the action is finished or complete. (This is called "completive" aspect.) Here are some examples of *pau* used as an auxiliary:

*You supposed to burn da Daruma dolls aftah you **pau** get your wish* . . . (Lum 1998b:224)
'You're supposed to burn the Daruma dolls after you've got your wish.'

*Jesus **pau** teach all dis kine story.* (DJB:43 [Matt.13:53])
'Jesus finished teaching all these kinds of stories.'

4.5.2.4 Combinations of auxiliaries, tense markers and modals

The auxiliaries *ste* (*stei, stay*) and *stat* (*start*) can co-occur with the tense markers. We've already seen examples above with *stat* following *wen* and *gon*. Here are examples with *ste*:

*De **gon ste** plei da gem tumaro.*
'They'll be playing the game tomorrow.'

*Hi **wen ste** it.*
'He was eating.'

This *wen + ste* construction is used in heavy Pidgin to indicate past progressive (indicated by *was/were V-ing* in English). Note that in past-tense constructions with *wen* in Pidgin, the *V-ing* form is not permitted. But in some varieties of Pidgin, the past progressive is marked with *waz* (*was*) rather than *wen + ste,* and this does use the *-ing* form of the verb:

*Yu **waz** iting mai sheiv ais*
'You were eating my shave ice.'

*. . . I **was** watching TV wit her.* (Lum 1998b:227)

Also in some varieties, *waz* (*was*) is used to show past tense before the future marker *gon* (*goin, going*) and the modal *sapostu* (*suppose to*):

*I **was going** lift weights wit Tommy Kono.* (Lum 1999:27)

*Last weekend I **was suppose to** go wit Vernalani folks to da Pure Heart concert.* (Kearns 2000:29)

Some of the modals can also occur before *ste* (*stei, stay*), but most often with the perfective meaning:

*Yu **sapostu ste** mek da rais awredi.*
'You were supposed to have made the rice.'

*Yu **kaen ste** mek evriting befo ai kam?*
'Can you have everything made before I come?'

4.5.2.5 Serial verbs

Two verbs, *go* and *kam* (*come*), can occur just before the main verb or before the auxiliary or before *chrai* (*try*). When they are used in this way, they are called "serial verbs" because they occur in a series with other verbs. A serial verb acts as an accessory to the main verb—with the role of contributing subtle nuances to its meaning or effect.

Serial verbs can have several functions. Most often, they indicate movement in space corresponding to the meanings of *go* and *kam* (*come*)—for example:

*We can **go find** dah treasure and take 'em.* (Pak 1998a:103)
'We can go and find the treasure and take it.'

***Go get** the hanger.* (Yamanaka 1998b:155)

*Mo bettah he **come play** handball wit us.* (Lum 1999:19–20)
'It'd be better if he came to play handball with us.'

*So da worka guys wen **go check out** all da roads.*
(DJB:66 [Matt.22:10])
'So the workers went to check out all the roads.'

*I going **come sit** on you.* (Lum 1998b:229)
'I'm gonna come and sit on you.'

Note that *go* or *kam* before the verb can itself be preceded by a tense marker—*wen* or *gon* (*goin, going*)—as in the preceding two examples.

Another related function of the serial verb *go* (but not *kam*) is that it can emphasize the intention involved in the action of the main verb (as with English *to go and do something*), implying that the person involved goes out of his or her way to do it:

*Wai yu **go du** daet?*
'Why did you go and do that?'

*Shi **go kuk** rais evri dei.*
'She goes and cooks rice every day.'

*So she <u>wen</u> **go hug** <u>him like that</u>.* (Labov 1990:28)
'So she went and hugged him like that.'

Again, when *go* is being used in this way, it can be preceded by a tense marker, as in the previous example.

The verb *go* before the main verb can also indicate movement in time—away from the present. So like the tense marker *gon* (*goin, going*), it can mark a future action or event, as in

*Ai **go kam** <u>tumaro</u>.*
'I'll come tomorrow.'

It is in this sense of movement away that *go* is used in some commands to indicate an action to be done elsewhere or later:

***Go color** <u>one eye fo me</u>.* (Lum 1998b:229)
'Color one eye for me.'

*<u>Try</u> **go read** <u>da Memoirs of the Hawaiian Revolution</u>.*
(Kearns 2000:30)
'Try reading the Memoirs of the Hawaiian Revolution.'

But with the serial verb *go,* in contrast to the the tense marker *gon* (*goin, going*), the action or event is usually one that has not been previously planned, is not so immediate, and may be more hypothetical than definite; in fact, the action might be intended but never take place:

*Mobeta wi **go tel** <u>hr</u>.*
'It would be better if we tell her.'

*I wen ask Fahdah Eugene fo **go pray** <u>fo you every day</u>.*
(Kearns 2000:34)
'I asked Father Eugene to pray for you every day.'

*Maybe das why he got all salty. Nobody pay attention to him. Nobody talk story with him. Nobody **go bother** him.* (Pak 1998b:321)
'Maybe that's why he got angry. Nobody paid attention to him. Nobody chatted with him. Nobody would bother him.'

*How one guy goin **go bus** inside one big moke house . . . ?* (DJB:36 [Matt.12:29])
'How will one guy go and break into a strong man's house . . . ?

Note that the serial verbs *go* and *kam* (*come*) occur only before active verbs, and not before stative verbs such as those that are followed by an AdjP (section 4.5.1), or others such as *no* (*know*) and *haev* (*have*).

4.5.2.6 Other combinations with serial verbs

We have already seen that serial verbs can be preceded by the tense markers *wen* and *gon* (*goin, going*). They can also be preceded by modals:

*I gotta **go rake**.* (Lum 1998b:71)
'I have to go rake.'

*We can **go find** dah treasure.* (Pak 1998a:103)
'Let's go and find the treasure.'

*You like **go see** one movie wit your dad?* (Kearns 2000:8))
'Do you want to go see a movie with your dad?'

In addition, serial verbs can occur either before or after auxiliaries. In the following examples, *go* occurs after the auxiliary *ste* (*stei, stay*), so that it is the combination of both the movement indicated by *go* plus the main verb that is seen as progressive:

*Shi **ste go bai** wan baeg rais.*
'She's going to buy a bag of rice.'

*Ai **ste go si** da gai.*
'I keep going to see the guy.'

In commands, *go* may come before the auxiliary *ste,* indicating a progressive or continuous action to be done elsewhere or later:

Go ste mek *da pupus.*
'Go on making the snacks.'

Go ste du *om.*
'Go keep doing it.'

Go can also come before the auxiliary when it has the function of indicating an unplanned future or hypothetical action, as in the second part of this famous Pidgin sentence:

Yu **go ste go***; ai* **go ste kam**. (*You* **go stay go***; I* **go stay come**.)
'You go ahead [i.e., keep going]; I'll be coming.'

The serial verb *go* can also occur before and after *chrai* (*try*):

Ai **go chrai du** *om fo yu.*
'I'll try to do it for you.'

Ai *laik* **chrai go kam mek** *kukiz wit yu.* (*I like* **try go come make** *cookies with you.*)
'I want to try to come and make cookies with you.'

Note that as shown in the preceding example, there may be two serial verbs used in one verb phrase. Here, *go* indicates an unplanned future action, and *kam* indicates motion toward the listener.

4.5.3 Summary

To summarize: We've seen that Pidgin has two different kinds of VPs: those with a stative main verb and those with an active main verb. (There are other types as well, covered in sections 5.2 and 5.7.)
Here is the structure of a VP with a stative main verb:

$$\text{VP} \rightarrow \text{(tense) (modal) } \textit{(chrai)} \text{ (auxiliary) V}_{\text{stative}} \quad \begin{matrix} \textbf{(AdjP)} \\ \textbf{or (NP)} \end{matrix} \quad \textbf{(PP)}$$

This means that a stative verb can occur on its own, but may also be preceded immediately by an auxiliary (*ste, stat,* or *pau*). A VP with a stative verb may begin with either a tense marker or a modal or both, which may be optionally followed by *chrai* (*try*). The stative verb can be followed by an optional AdjP or NP, and an optional PP.

Here is the structure of a VP with an active main verb (where "sv" indicates the possible positions for a serial verb):

$$\text{VP} \rightarrow \text{(tense) (modal) (sv) } \textit{(chrai)} \text{ (sv) (auxiliary) (sv) V}_{\text{active}} \text{ (NP) (PP)}$$

The difference is that the active verb may be preceded by a serial verb, and is not followed by an AdjP.

These two types of VP are illustrated in the following diagram. (Note that not all combinations are possible.)

(wen) (gon) (yustu)	(kaen) (laik) (haeftu) (sapostu) (gata) (beta)	(go) (kam)	(chrai)	(go) (kam)	(ste) (stat) (pau)	(go) (kam)	stative main verb or active main verb	(AdjP) (NP)	(PP)

Also note that *waz* (*was*) is not included in these diagrams. It can occur in the following environments: before the tense marker *gon*, before the modal *sapostu*, or before the *-ing* form of an active main verb (with the restrictions described above).

There's one word class or phrase that can also appear in the VP that has been left out of these diagrams—the adverb or AdvP. We've already seen that an adverb or AdvP can occur at the end of the VP. It can also occur before the VP or before the PP at the end of the VP—but not in the "core" of the VP. The constituents of the core are shown in the shaded area below. An adverb or AdvP of time, such as *evritaim* (*everytime*), can occur where there are double lines.

(wen) *(gon)* *(yustu)*	*(kaen)* *(laik)* *(haeftu)* *(sapostu)* *(gata)* *(beta)*	*(go)* *(kam)*	*(chrai)*	*(go)* *(kam)*	*(ste)* *(stat)* *(pau)*	*(go)* *(kam)*	stative main verb or active main verb	*(AdjP)* *(NP)*	*(PP)*

Other kinds of adverbs or AdvPs, however, have a more restricted distribution.

Finally, note that a VP can be shortened in some contexts so that it contains just a tense marker or just a modal, such as *Hi yustu* (*He used to*) or *Ai kaen* (*I can*).

4.5.4 More on the tense system of Pidgin

In English, there's an unmarked form of the verb—for example: *eat, work, pass, run, think,* etc. Usually we think of this as the present tense form—as in sentences such as *I eat four meals a day* or *My friends work downtown.* But this form can also be used for actions that take place in the future or in the past. For example, you could say: *I go to Vegas next week.* Or a newspaper headline might read: *Legislators pass seatbelt law* (referring to something that happened in the past). Furthermore, in narratives, we can use what's called the "historical present"—that is, present tense forms of the verb while talking about the past—for example: *Last week I'm sitting in the park and these guys come up and start hassling me.*

Pidgin also uses the unmarked form of the verb to talk about things that happen in the present, future, or past, and also in the historical present, but these are much more common in Pidgin than in English, and so the unmarked verb is used far more often.

When English does use past tense, it shows it with the suffix *-ed* on regular verbs or some change in form for irregular verbs. In contrast Pidgin uses a preceding tense marker—*wen* (or *bin* or *haed*)—so the form of the actual verb does not change. For example, compare English *sing/sang* to Pidgin *sing/wen sing.*

However, Pidgin does use a few English irregular verb forms to show past tense. The most common is *sed* (*said*). (It is rare to hear *wen sei.*) Others are *sin* (*seen*) or *saw, keim* (*came*), and *tol* (*told*). (These occur in variation with w*en si, wen kam,* and *wen tel.*) When these forms are used, they do not normally occur with the past tense marker *wen* (or *bin* or *haed*). Some examples are

> *Shi **sed** shi wen smok om. (She **said** she wen smoke em.)*
> 'She said she smoked it.'

> *Hi **tol** om, No.*
> 'He told him, No.'

> *Shi **sin** wan sigaret. (She **seen** one cigarette.)*
> 'She saw a cigarette.'

(The use of *sin* (*seen*) is a relatively recent innovation in Pidgin.)

There are some other major differences between the past tense systems of English and Pidgin. When past tense is used in an English narrative, almost every verb must be marked (with -*ed* or a changed form of the verb). But when past tense is used in a Pidgin narrative, only some verbs are marked—for example:

> He **went wink** *at me and tell, "Choo, choo, choo" and laugh back-*
> *wards, you know like he sucking air in, "Hurh, hurh, hurh."*
> (Lum 1999:26)
> 'He **winked** at me and **said**, "Choo, choo, choo" and **laughed** back-
> wards, you know like he **was sucking** air in, "Hurh, hurh, hurh."

This is because in Pidgin, once the past time frame is established by marking one verb for past tense, it isn't necessary to mark the verbs that follow.

Also, the past tense in Pidgin is often "relative." This means that it is used only to indicate something that had occurred previously in relation to the actual time being discussed. So if an event happened before another event—that is, even further in the past—then the past tense marker is used. For example, the following sentence comes from a narrative of past events:

*Da Man/Lady stay piss off dat I **went change** da channel.*
(Lum 1999:27)
'The man/lady was pissed off that I had changed the channel.'

Because of the influence of English, where everything that occurred in the past must be marked, some Pidgin speakers, and especially writers, use the past tense marker *wen* more frequently:

*Dat time nobody **wen** bodda da peopo dat **wen** come togedda for church all ova Judea, Galilee an Samaria. Dey **wen** trus God mo an mor and God's Spesho Spirit **wen** kokua dem.* (DJB:337 [Acts 9:31]).

'At that time nobody bothered the people that came together for church all over Judea, Galilee and Samaria. They trusted God more and more and God's Special Spirit helped them.'

Differences also exist between the future tense systems of English and Pidgin. In English, the future markers *will* or *is/are going to* are used only to mark an action or event that will take place in the absolute future—that is, at a time after the statement is made. If you're talking about a statement regarding the future that someone made in the past, then you can use *will* or *is/are going to* if the action or event hasn't occurred yet. But if it has occurred, you have to use *would* or *was/were going to*. For example, these two sentences both imply that the action hasn't been done yet:

He said that he will do it.
He said that he is going to do it.

So you couldn't say: **He said that he will do it and he did it.* You'd have to say:

He said that he would do it and he did it. or
He said that he was going to do it, and he did it.

In Pidgin, however, the future tense marker *gon* (*goin, going*) can be used to mark not only actions that will occur in the absolute future, but also future actions being talked about in the past that may have occurred already—for example:

*When I went Farrington, brah, you no can talk Pidgin, you **going** run home every day from school.* (Kearns 2000:32)

'When I went to Farrington [High School], brother, if you couldn't speak in Pidgin, you would [have to] run home from school everyday.'

*Da gai sed hi **gon** fiks mi ap wit wan blain deit.*

'The guy said he'd fix me up with a blind date.'

But some Pidgin speakers use *waz* (*was*) to mark such past-future constructions:

*He said dat she **was going** help all us guys go heaven.*

(Lum 1998b:225)

Chapter 5

Types of Sentences

Pidgin has two basic types of sentences: those with a verb phrase (VP) and those without. Sentences can also be grouped into other different categories: probability, negative, imperative, questions, exclamations, and those with discourse particles. Finally, the basic form of various sentences can be changed to emphasize or focus on certain aspects.

5.1 Sentences with a noun phrase and a verb phrase

The most common sentences in Pidgin have a noun phrase (NP) followed by a verb phrase (VP), just like in English. Nearly all the example sentences in section 4.5 about the VP are of this type, with the initial NP not underlined and the VP underlined. So the structure of this type of sentence is as follows (where S stands for "sentence"):

S → NP VP

Here's another example (one that we've seen already):

Da worka guys <u>wen go check out all da roads</u>. (DJB:66 [Matt.22:10]) 'The workers went and checked out all the roads.'

The initial NP is *Da worka guys,* and the VP is *wen go check out all da roads*. Notice that the VP is made up of the tense marker *wen,* the serial verb *go,* the main verb (a phrasal verb) *check out,* and the NP *all the roads,* which is part of the VP.

In sentences like this, the first NP of the sentence is called the "subject," and the NP that's part of the verb phrase (i.e., that comes after the verb) is called the "object." (Of course not all VPs have an NP, and so not all sentences have an object. For example:

His girlfriend gatta work tonight.
'His girlfriend has to work tonight.'

My brada stay sleeping inside da house.
'My brother is sleeping in the house.'

In the second sentence above, there is an NP *da house* which comes after the verb *sleeping,* but it is part of a prepositional phrase *inside da house,* so it doesn't come right after the verb, and therefore doesn't count as the object of the sentence.

5.2 Sentences with just a verb phrase

In English, almost all sentences have a subject NP. The exceptions are "imperatives," or commands, such as *Clean your room!* or *Open the door.* In Pidgin too, imperative sentences do not usually have a subject NP (see section 5.7). But Pidgin has many other kinds of sentences that have only a VP. These sentences have the structure

S → VP

For example, "existential" sentences (sentences beginning with *there is, there was,* etc., in English) do not have a subject in Pidgin:

Nonpast existential ('there is/are') sentences usually begin with the verb *get*:

Get *wan nu bilding ova dea.*
'There's a new building over there.'

Get *plenty time.* (Lum 1998b:227)
'There's plenty of time.'

Get *two problems wit dat translation.* (Kearns 2000:27)
'There are two problems with that translation.'

Past existential ("there was/were") sentences begin with *haed* (*had*):

Had *dis old green house . . .*
'There was this old green house . . . '] (Lum 1990:60)

Had *some Pharisee guys . . .* (DJB:56 [Matt.19:3])
'There were some Pharisees . . . '

Note that unlike the verb phrases covered in section 4.5, the verb phrase in existential sentences does not have tense markers, modals, auxiliaries or serial verbs preceding the main verb.

In sentences such as *It's raining,* English uses the "dummy subject" *it* (which doesn't really refer to anything). Pidgin doesn't require any dummy subject:

Gon ren tumaro.
'It's going to rain tomorrow.'

Also, like many other languages (but not English), Pidgin does not need a pronoun subject NP (*Ai, yu, hi, shi, it, wi, de*) when the identity of the subject is clear from the context or previous utterances, for example:

Wen tawk tu om yestade.
'I talked to him yesterday.'

Like beef?
'You want to fight?'

Ste chraing fo ak lokol.
'He's trying to act local.'

Subjectless sentences for some speakers of Pidgin may begin with the linking verb *iz* (*is*) or *waz* (*was*):

Is really nice.
'It is really nice.'

Was boring.
'It was boring.'

5.3 Sentences without objects or prepositions

There are some other differences between Pidgin and English sentences with VPs. First, for some verbs, Pidgin (unlike English) does not require an object (especially *it*) when its identity is clear from the context:

I wen give you.
'I gave it to you.'

Ai no kaen handol.
'I can't handle it.'

No foget teik.
'Don't forget to take some.'

Second, in some sentences giving locations, the location may be given without a preposition such as *at, to, on* or *in*. (In such cases, the location is acting as an adverb of place.) Here are some examples:

Lucky you live Hawai'i.
'Lucky that you live in Hawai'i.'

George wen go Vegas.
'George went to Las Vegas.'

Hiz haus ste da mauka said.
'His house is on the mountain side.'

As gaiz kaen go pati yo haus.
'We can go party at your house.'

5.4 Sentences without a verb phrase ("verbless" sentences)

Nearly all sentences in English have a VP, but there are some exceptions, such as *The more the merrier.* But many languages, including Pidgin, have various types of sentences without a VP (known as "verbless" sentences). Here we will look at three different types.

5.4.1 Equational sentences

The first types of verbless sentences are called "equational sentences." They are usually formed just by joining two noun phrases and do not require a linking verb (*am, is, are, was, were*) as English does. Therefore they have the structure **S → NP NP**.

Mai sista wan bas jraiva.
'My sister is a bus driver.'

Nau yu da baws.
'Now you're the boss.'

Da buk mainz.
'The book is mine.'

A very common type of equational sentence uses the demonstrative pronouns *daes* (*dass, das*) or *aes* (*as*) meaning 'that's':

Daes mai pen.
'That's my pen.'

And das the one by my house . . . (Pak 1998a:108)
'And that's the one by my house.'

Aes wai.
'That's why.'

Some speakers, however, use *iz* (*is*) or *waz* (*was*) as a linking verb:

Brynie is da Captain. (Lum 1998b:223)
'Brynie is the Captain.'

He was one old guy. (Lum 1999:22)
'He was an old guy.'

5.4.2 Sentences with an adjective phrase (AdjP)

The second type of verbless sentence is made up of an AdjP and an NP. In such sentences the AdjP may come after the NP or before the NP, and no linking verb is required.

First we'll look at sentences in which the person/thing being described (the NP) comes first and the AdjP second. The structure is **S → NP AdjP**:

Mai sista skini.
'My sister is skinny.'

Da buggah brown. (Morales 1988:72)
'The guy's brown.'

Da old wine mo betta. (DJB:174 [Luke 5:39])
'The old wine is better.'

Sentences with the AdjP second can also use the demonstrative pronouns *daes* (*dass, das*) or *aes* (*as*) meaning 'that's':

Daes rait.
'That's right.'

Aes mo waws.
'That's worse.'

Also, as we've seen in the discussion of the verb phrase (section 4.5.1), the Pidgin linking verb *ste* (*stei, stay*) may also be used before AdjPs. But it can only be used before adjectives or AdjPs that denote a nonpermanent or nonintrinsic quality, or a change in conditions—for example:

*hi **stey** free eswy.* (bradajo 1998a:19)
'He's free, that's why.'

*Shi **stei** sik.*
'She is sick.'

But the following is not acceptable because the adjective denotes a permanent quality:

Da wahine ste shawt.
'The woman is short.'

Again, some speakers of lighter Pidgin use *iz* (*is*) or *waz* (*was*) as a linking verb before the AdjP, as is required in English:

*His one **is** cool.* (Tonouchi 1998:251)

*Tommy Kono **was** short.* (Lum 1999:23)

Verbless sentences with an AdjP can also have the AdjP first, followed by the NP. The structure is therefore **S → AdjP NP**:

Ono da malasadaz.
'The malasadas are delicious.'

Too long da words. (Kearns 2000:21)
'The words are too long.'

In such sentences a linking verb is not normally used.

5.4.3 Locational sentences

The last type of verbless sentence is the kind that gives a location, with either an adverb or a prepositional phrase. So its structure is either

S → NP AdvP or **S → NP PP**.

In sentences where the location is *here* or *there* or where there's a phrase giving the location, no linking verb is needed:

Mai sista hia.
'My sister is here.'

Kent dem insaid da haus.
'Kent and the others are inside the house.'

Similarly, *wea* (*where*) questions do not need a linking verb:

Eh, wea dis guy from? (DJB:23[Matt.8:27])
'Hey, where's this guy from?'

But where dah bridge? (Pak 1998a:113)
'But where's the bridge?'

But the linking verb *ste* (*stei*, *stay*) can also be used with locations. With *hia* (*here*) or *dea* (*dere*, *there*), it can mean 'stay' as in English:

He always stay dere and hog da TV. (Lum 1999:26)
'He always stays there and hogs the TV.'

He stay inside da coffin. (Lum 1999:26)
'He's inside the coffin.'

Where he stay? (Ching 1998:183)
'Where is he?'

5.5 Probability sentences

Probability sentences are those that comment on the likelihood of the occurrence of an event, action, or state of affairs. In Pidgin there are two probability markers, which usually occur at the beginning of the sentence. First, *mebi* (*maybe*) indicates that the speaker thinks that there is a possibility that the action or event will take place or has taken place, or that what's stated in the rest of the sentence is true:

Maybe *I no undastand afta all.* (Kearns 2000:24)
'Maybe I don't understand after all.'

Maybe *das why dey come fat.* (Lum 1999:20)
'Maybe that's why they get fat.'

For us, dat jes means dat da tree going die, or ***maybe*** *stay dead awreaddy.* (Lum 1998a:71)

'For us, that just means that the tree is going to die or maybe is dead already.'

Second, *masbi* (*mus be*, *must be*) indicates the belief that some action or event has most probably occurred or a particular state of affairs exists. The way it's used in Pidgin is similar to expressions in English such as *It must be . . .* or *It must be that . . .* ; however, the anticipatory *it* and the following *that* are not used in Pidgin:

> ***Must be*** *buried right ovah there.* (Pak 1998a:111)
> 'It must be buried right over there.'

> *She just started giggling.* ***Must be*** *my shoes I tot.* (Tonouchi 1998:250)
> 'She just started giggling. It must be my shoes, I thought.'

> ***Masbi*** *hi laik da lanch. Hi it om awl ap.*
> 'It must be that he liked the lunch. He ate it all up.'

5.6 Negative sentences

In Pidgin, sentences are made negative by using one of four negative markers: *nat, no, neva,* and *nomo.* Here Pidgin is much more complex than English, which has only one negative marker, *not* (or the contracted form *n't*). In a Pidgin sentence with a VP, the negative marker is placed before the tense marker, modal, auxiliary, serial verb, or main verb, whichever comes first. In a verbless sentence, it is placed before the second phrase—the NP, AdjP, AdvP, or PP. Again, this is more complicated than in English, where sentences are always made negative by inserting the word *not* after an auxiliary such as *did, is,* or *were,* or after a modal such as *will* or *can.*

The four Pidgin negative markers are used in the following contexts:

Nat (*not*) is used in four situations: (1) before the NP, AdjP, AdvP, or PP in verbless sentences; (2) before the tense marker *gon* (*goin, going, gonna*); (3) before the *-ing* form of the verb when it's not preceded by *ste* (*stei, stay*); and (4) before the modal *sapostu*:

*Mai sista **nat** wan bas jraiva.*
'My sister isn't a bus driver.'

*Da buga **nat** braun.*
'The guy isn't brown.'

*Hi **nat** goin brok om.*
'He's not going to break it.'

*Da gaiz **nat** wrking.*
'The guys aren't working.'

*Yu **nat** sapostu du daet.*
'You're not supposed to do that.'

Nat (*not*) also occurs with the modal *beta* but the order is reversed:

*Yu beta **nat** du daet.*
'You'd better not do that.'

No is used in six situations: (1) before the plain, unmarked verb; (2) before the tense marker *gon* (*goin, going, gonna*); (3) before the modals *kaen, laik, gata,* and *haeftu*; (4) before the linking verb *ste* (*stei, stay*); (5) before the auxiliaries *ste* (*stei, stay*), *stat,* and *pau*; and (6) before the serial verbs *go* and *kam* (*come*).

*Da kaet **no** it fish.*
'The cat doesn't each fish.'

*I **no** goin tell nobody.* (DJB:2 [Matt.1:19])
'I won't tell anybody.'

*I **no** can even do twenty [pushups] in da P.E. test in school.*
(Lum 1999:22)
'I can't even do twenty [pushups] in the P.E. test in school.'

*I **no** like flunk.* (Kearns 2000:11)
'I don't want to flunk.'

*Kaerol **no** haeftu wrk.*
'Carol doesn't have to work.'

*Da kaet **no** ste in da haus.*
'The cat isn't in the house.'

*Hi **no** ste sik.*
'He isn't sick.'

*I like pau by tonight, even if it mean I **no** go sleep.* (Kearns 2000:26)
'I want to finish tonight even if it means I don't sleep.'

*De **no** ste lisining.*
'They aren't listening.'

*Mai sista **no** stat pleing saka.* 'My sister hasn't started playing soccer.'

*Ai **no** pau kuk da rais yet.* 'I haven't finished cooking the rice yet.'

You may have noticed that either *nat* or *no* can be used before the tense marker *gon* (*goin, going, gonna*), but for some speakers, there's a slight difference: *nat* implies a contradiction or change—for example:

No *gon ren tumaro.* 'It's not going to rain tomorrow.'
Nat *gon ren tumaro.* 'It's not going to rain tomorrow (even though you think it is).'

*Shi **no** gon plei saka.* 'She's not going to play soccer.'
*Shi **nat** gon plei saka.* 'She's not going to play soccer (now that she's changed her mind).'

Also, note that *nat* is quite often used before *pau*, but this is when *pau* is being used an adjective meaning 'finished', rather than as an auxiliary or a verb.

*Ai **nat** pau yet.*
'I'm not finished yet.'

*Neva (**nevah, never**)* is used before the verb or auxiliary to indicate negative and past tense at the same time:

*Ai **neva** du om.*
'I didn't do it.'

*He **nevah** say nutting.* (Lum 1999:24)
'He didn't say anything.'

*De **neva** ste lisin.*
'They weren't listening.'

*De **neva** pau teik da tes.*
'They didn't finish taking the test.'

Neva is also used before the tense marker *yustu* (*use to*):

*She **nevah** use to have one big fat turkey fo Tanksgiving.*
(Lum 1998a:74)
'She didn't used to have a big fat turkey for Thanksgiving.'

Note that *no wen* is not normally used for past tense negative, and that *neva* (*nevah, never*) does not simply mean 'not ever' as it does in English. For example, the meaning of *I never eat beans* in Pidgin is 'I didn't eat beans', not 'I don't ever eat beans'.

*Nomo (**no more**)*, the final negative, is different from the others in that it is not used before a verb or modal or auxiliary. Rather, it occurs before an NP in a subjectless sentence to mark negative nonpast existential—i.e., meaning 'there isn't' or 'there aren't'.

Nomo kaukau in da haus.
'There isn't any food in the house.'

It also is used in a negative possessive sentence to mean 'doesn't have' or 'don't have':

*Nau wi **nomo** ka.*
'Now we don't have a car.'

*How come I **no more** one real glove?* (Chock 1998:29)
'How come I don't have a real glove?'

Two other expressions are also sometimes used for negative possessive: *no haev* (*no have*) and *no get*.

Nomo can be used to talk about things in the past—for example:

*We **no more** their kind money.* (Kono 1998:210)
'We didn't have their kind of money.'

But other expressions can also be used—i.e., *no haed* (*no had*), *neva haed*
(*never had*), *neva haev* (*never have*), and *neva get* (*never get*):

Neva haed TV.
'There wasn't any TV.'

Different negatives are used on their own in answer to different kinds
of questions:

No is used as in English for disagreement.

You goin surf tomorrow?   No.

Nat is used for contradiction or denial:

You gon flunk yoa class?   Nat! (i.e., 'No, I'm not!')

Nomo is used to say something doesn't exist or you don't have something:

You get some money?   Nomo. (i.e., 'No, I don't have any.')

Other forms of negatives:

Other forms of negatives are used by some Pidgin speakers.

First there is the set expression *dono* or *donno* (*dunno*), which, like its English origin, means 'don't know' or 'doesn't know':

*I **donno** why he no leave um on.* (Lum 1999:20)
'I don't know why he doesn't leave it on.'

*I **dunno** who wen' tell my madda.* (Yamanaka 1998b:156)
'I don't know who told my mother.'

*Shi **dono** was haepening.*
'She doesn't know what's happening.'

For speakers who use *waz* (*was*) as a tense marker or auxiliary, the negative markers *no* or *neva* can be used with it:

*Shi **no** waz going.*
'She wasn't going.'

*Ai wen go fo si om yestadie, but hi **neva** waz home.*
'I went to see him yesterday, but he wasn't home.'

Forms of negatives closer to English are used by speakers of lighter varieties of Pidgin. These include: *kaenat* (*cannot*), *don* (*don't*), *diden* (*didn't*), *izen* (*isn't*), *wazen* (*wasn't*), and *won* (*won't*).

So-called "double negatives":

Like many other languages, Pidgin can use a negative marker on both the verb and the noun or noun phrase—for example:

*Shi **neva** bring **no** kaukau.*
'She didn't bring any food.'

*De **no** du **nating**.*
'They didn't do anything,'

***Nomo nating** insai dea.*
'There isn't anything in there.'

*Ai **no** kaen si **nobadi**.*
'I can't see anybody.'

*Hi **no** go **nopleis**.*
'He doesn't go anywhere.'

5.7 Imperatives

In imperatives, the verb appears first in the sentence, as in English:

Come wit me. (Kearns 2000:9)
'Come with me.'

Bring om baek wen yu pau, ae?
'Bring it back when you finish, OK?'

However, unlike in English, *chrai* (*try*) is used to soften commands, as a kind of politeness marker (although not as strong as *please*):

***Chrai** paes da rais.*
'Could you pass the rice.'

*Faye, **try** wait!* (Kearns 2000:28)
'Faye, wait a minute!'

*Terry, **try** look what I found!* (Pak 1998a:101)
'Terry, have a look at what I found!'

Negative imperatives (prohibitives) are formed by putting *no* before the verb:

***No** mek fan.*
'Don't make fun.'

5.8 Questions

Questions in both Pidgin and English are of two types. First are "yes/no questions," which can be answered by either "yes" or "no"—for example, in English: *Are you going to the party?* or *Did he get that job?* Second are "information questions," which use one of the question words, in English: *who, what, which, where, when, why,* and *how*—for example, *Who is that guy? What are you doing? Where did they go?* (These are sometimes called "wh questions" because of the spelling of most of the question words.)

5.8.1 Yes/no questions

In English, yes/no questions usually have a special form in which the order of the subject and the auxiliary or modal is reversed—for example: statement: *The boys were playing baseball.* question: *Were the boys playing baseball?* If there is no auxiliary, one is inserted for the question—for example: statement: *They live in Kalihi.* question: *Do they live in Kalihi?* In Pidgin, however, an auxiliary or modal is not needed for a question, and even if there is one, word order does not change. But in spoken Pidgin, there is a very distinct questioning intonation (see section 2.5.4). Some examples of yes/no questions in Pidgin are

You going da game? (Lum 1998b:225)
'Are you going to the game?'

You like come? (Ching 1998:182)
'Do you want to come?'

Ai kaen plei?
'Can I play?'

5.8.2 Information questions

Pidgin uses information question words similar to those of English: *wat* (*what*), *wich* (*which*), *hu* (*who*), *huz* (*whose*), *wea* (*where*), *wen* (*when*), *wai* (*why*), and *hau* (*how*). As in English, the question word occurs first in the sentence, but again, in Pidgin there is no need for an auxiliary or change in word order. Here are some examples:

What *you looking at?* (Kanae 1998:208)
'What are you looking at?'

Which one you like me let go? (DJB:88 [Matt.27:21])
'Which one do you want me to let go?'

Who going watch my back? (Ching 1998:189)
'Who's going to watch my back?'

Who dat? (Kearns 2000:5)
'Who is that?'

Whose treasure dis? (Pak 1998a:102)
'Whose treasure is this?'

Where you going wit dat? (Kearns 2000:8)
'Where are you going with that?'

When you going come back and lift weights wit me? (Lum 1999:27)
'When will you come back and lift weights with me?'

Why you like be something you not? (Kono 1998:211)
'Why do you want to be something you're not?'

How you know? (Ching 1998:187)
'How do you know?'

Note that *hau mach* (*how much*) can be used where *how many* is used in English:

How much baskets you guys wen pick up afta? (DJB:49 [Matt.16:9])
'How many baskets did you pick up afterwards?'

Often, two-word question words are used, such as *wat taim* (*what time*) 'when', *hau kam* (*how come*) 'why', *wat fo* (*what for*) 'why', and '*wat kain*' (*what kind of*):

Wat time all dat kine stuff goin happen? (DJB:73 [Matt.24:3])
'When will all those kinds of things happen?'

How come *I no more one real glove?* (Chock 1998:28)
'Why don't I have a real glove?'

Wat fo *yu laik bai daet?*
'Why do you want to buy that?'

Wat kain *fud yu laik it?*
'What kind of food do you like to eat?'

Another Pidgin question word is *was* (*whas, what's*), meaning 'what is' or 'what's':

Whas *dis?* (Pak 1998a:102)
'What's this?'

Wa's *da last ting you rememba?* (Kearns 2000:6)
'What's the last thing you remember?'

5.9 Exclamations

Exclamations are sentences in which surprise or some other emotion is forcefully expressed, such as *Oh, that's terrible!*, *Wow, look at that!* and *What a beautiful baby!* As in English, exclamations in Pidgin usually begin with interjections (section 3.13). Here are some examples:

Oh, *tank you, docta.* (Kearns 2000:5)
'Oh, thank you, doctor.'

Ho, *your boy, big boy, eh?* (Lum 1999:19)
'Gee, your boy is a big boy, isn't he?'

Ho, *he really crack me up!* (Kearns 2000:27)
'Man, he really cracked me up.'

Eh, *no mo one Latin word fo gecko!* (Kearns 2000:22)
'Hey, there's no Latin word for gecko!'

Eh, *no fut around!* (Pak 1998b:321)
'Hey, don't fart around!'

Ho ka*! Awesome, yeah?* (DJB:73 [Matt.24:01])
'Wow! Awesome, isn't it?'

Auwe*! You one real poho worka!* (DJB:78 [Matt.25:26])
'Oh dear! You're a really useless worker!'

Hala*! Yu gon get it nau!*
'Now you've done it! You're going to get it now!

Pidgin also has a unique kind of exclamation in which the adjective is preceded by the article *da*:

Oh, ***da*** *cute!*
'Oh, how cute!'

Ho da *scary!* (Lum 1999:21)
'Oh, that's scary!'

Ho, ***da*** *hat!*
'Yikes, it's hot!'

Such exclamations can also use the Hawaiian article *ka* in place of *da*, as in

Ho, ka *priti.*
'Oh, how pretty!'

Note that interjections can also be used for emphasis in sentences that are not exclamations:

*I no mind but **ho**, she like talk to all da old fogies on da bus.*
(Lum 1998:226).
'I didn't mind but, man, she liked to talk to all the old fogies on the bus.'

*But **eh**! I telling you guys dis. No fight back da bad guys.*
(DJB:14 [Matt.5:39])
'But, hey, I'm telling you guys this. Don't fight back against the bad guys.'

5.10 Sentences with discourse particles

The Pidgin discourse particles—*yae* (*yeah*), *ae* (*eh*), *ha* (*huh*), and *no*—were listed in section 3.14. These are a very distinctive feature of Pidgin and are used quite frequently by some speakers. They have four different functions.

First, discourse particles may be used as confirmation checks, much like the "question tags" that are used at the end of sentences in English, such as *isn't it?*, *didn't they?*, or *won't you?*

*Dis rum TP 101, **ae**?*
'This is room TP 101, isn't it?'

*Wi gon finish, **no**?*
'We're going to finish, aren't we?'

*You Cowboy's numbah two boy, **yeah**?* (Lum 1999:23)
'You're Cowboy's second son, aren't you?'

*I guess nowdays cannot tell from lass name, **no**?* (Tonouchi 1998:252)
'I guess nowadays you can't tell from the last name, can you?'

*But he nevah say had one fishpond or not, **eh**, ovah there?*
(Pak 1998a:111)
'But he didn't say whether or not there was a fishpond over there, did he?'

Second, discourse particles may have a facilitative function—to get a conversation started or keep it going by involving the listener. In English, this is done with question tags or fillers such as *you know?*, *you follow?*, *right?*, or *eh?*

*So wi giv da gai da haus, **ae**?*
'So we give the guy the house, right?'

*Funny, **yeah**.* (Lum 1999:22)
'Funny, isn't it?'

*He talk slow, **eh**, cuz ninety-two, him.* (Kearns 2000:21)
'He talks slow, you know, because he's ninety-two.'

She one witch, yeah? (Lum 1998b:222)
'She's a witch, you know?'

*Maybe dat too, **no**?* (Kearns 2000:34)
'Maybe that too, eh?'

Third, discourse particles may function to soften a comment. In other words, they may be used so that a comment doesn't sound so strong or abrupt.

*Sorry, **eh**?* (Kearns 2000:17)

*No laugh, **eh**?* (Kearns 2000:24)

*Das so sweet **yeah**.* (Tonouchi 1998:250)

Fourth, discourse particles sometimes have a confrontational function, as question tags do in English:

*You tink you one tough blala, **eh**?* (Kearns 2000:31)
'You think you're a tough guy, don't you?'

5.11 Focusing

Languages normally have ways to focus on or emphasize a particular part of a sentence, and Pidgin is no exception. This is done by adding particular extra words or by moving bits to the beginning or end of the sentence.

One way of focusing on the subject of a sentence is to follow it with a pronoun referring to the same subject—for example:

Mai fada, **hi** *no laik go wrk.*
'My father didn't like to go to work.'

. . . my sista, **she** *the boss of the sunflower seeds.*
(Yamanaka 1998a:153)
' . . . my sister was the boss of the sunflower seeds.'

Weightlifters, **dey** *no do too much.* (Lum 1999:19)
'Weightlifters don't do too much.'

Eh, you know, dem guys, **dey** *ack so wild, jalike dey crazy.*
(DJB:23 [Matt.8:28])
'Hey, you know, those guys act so wild, just like they're crazy.'

Another way to focus on a part of a sentence is to follow it with a discourse particle—usually *ae, yae (yeah)*, or *e (eh)*—for example:

Mai kidz, **ae**, *awlweiz kritisaizing mi.*
'My kids, you know, they're always criticizing me.'

Sometimes both strategies (pronoun and discourse particle) are used at once:

As gaiz bifo, **ae**, **wi** *no it California rais.*
'Previously we didn't eat California rice.'

Another strategy for focusing on a part of a sentence is to move it to the beginning. This is possible in English—for example, *That movie, I really liked*—but it is much more common in Pidgin. In the following examples, the object is moved to the beginning of the sentence:

Pleni mani hi get.
'He has a lot of money.'

Onli da jank kain hi let yu teik.
'He lets you take only ones that aren't any good.'

Dat wan ai si.
'I see that one.'

There can also be double focusing, involving both movement and following the subject with a pronoun:

*Enikain fud dis gai **hi** it.*
'All kinds of food, this guy eats.'

When the object or location is moved, a pronoun or adverb may be inserted in its original place, sometimes where it is not required in English:

*Dis wan ai wen bai **om** Longs.*
'This one I bought at Longs.'

*Dis glove, you try bend **um**, no can.* (Chock 1998:28)
'This glove, if you try to bend it, you can't.'

*At da Y get plenny guys living **ovah dere** in da upstairs rooms.*
(Lum 1999:25)
'At the Y, there are lots of guys living in the upstairs rooms.'

A discourse particle is also sometimes used to focus on the moved part of the sentence:

*Mai kantri, **yae**? Niigata, foa mans sno.*
(*My country, **yeah**? Niigata, four months snow.*)
'In my country, Niigata, it snows for four months.'

*Every place da bugga go, he stay smiling, cuz white, **eh**, his teeth.*
(Kearns 2000:31)
'Every place the guys goes, he smiles—because his teeth are white, you know.'

English uses movement for focus in constructions such *It was the butler who did it*. Such constructions are found in Pidgin as well, in sentences beginning with *waz* (*was*):

Waz as gaiz hu wen laik go.
'It was us who wanted to go.'

Movement can also be used in Pidgin for "defocusing." Here, when the speaker does not want to focus on the subject, or when it is an afterthought, it is moved to the end of the sentence:

Get pleni mani, yu.
'You have a lot of money.'

No laik plei futbawl, diz gaiz.
'These guys don't like to play football.'

Geting ol, as gaiz.
'We're getting old.'

No laik it nating, dis gai.
'This guy doesn't like to eat anything.'

In such cases, the part that remains after the subject is moved to the end and may be followed by the discourse particle *ae* (*eh*):

*No mo sach ting aez Krismas **ae**? as gaiz.*
(*No mo such thing as Christmas **eh**? us guys.*)
'There's no such thing as Christmas for us.'

*Moningtaim gud **ae**? fishing.*
(*Morningtime good **eh**? fishing.*)
'Morning is a good time for fishing.'

In addition, a sentence can have both focusing and defocusing, by moving the object to the beginning of the sentence, and the subject to the end.

In such sentences, a pronoun is inserted in the original place of the defocused subject (which has been moved to the end).

*Pleni mani **de** get, sam gaiz.*
'Some guys have a lot of money.'

(For more information on sentences with discourse particles and focusing, see Perlman 1973.)

Chapter 6

Complex Sentences

Complex sentences are those that are made up of more than one sentence. (The sentences that make up a complex sentence are called "clauses.") Take, for example, the complex sentence *Jessie came to town but Fred stayed at home.* This is made up of two clauses: *Jessie came to town* and *Fred stayed at home.* They are joined by a "conjunction," *but.*

One of the clauses in a complex sentence may be only part of a longer sentence, or changed in some way. For example, in *I bumped into my friend who's a pilot,* the two clauses are actually *I bumped into my friend* and *My friend's a pilot.*

Here we'll look at three types of complex sentences: those involving coordination, those involving subordination, and those involving direct quotations. Then we'll look at sentences linked by connectors (which are not really complex sentences because they remain separate from each other).

6.1 Coordination

In complex sentences involving "coordination," each of the clauses has equal importance, and can often stand on its own. Coordinate sentences in Pidgin are similar to those in English, and normally use one of three "coordinating conjunctions" to join the clauses: *aen* (*an, and*), *aen den* (*an den, and then*), *bat* (*but*), or *o* (*or*):

He eat grasshopper, ***an*** *he get honey from da bees.* (DJB:5 [Matt.3:4])
'He ate grasshoppers, and he got honey from the bees.'

He always lift little bit ***and den*** *he do situps.* (Lum 1999:22)
'He always lifts a little bit and then he does pushups.'

*Nobody like listen, **but** she went say um already.* (Lum 1998b:227)
'Nobody wanted to listen, but she said it already.'

*Usually da TV stay on **or** my grandpa stay listening to his Japanese radio station.* (Tonouchi 1998:245)
'Usually the TV is on or my grandpa is listening to his Japanese radio station.'

Pidgin is similar to some dialects of English (such as Australian English) in that *bat* (*but*) can occur either before the second clause (as above) or at the end of the second clause (as below):

*I no like you, brudda. I no can tell you how come, **but**.*
(Kearns 2000:30)
'I don't like you, brother, but I can't tell you why.'

6.2 Subordination

In complex sentences involving "subordination," the two clauses are not of equal importance. Instead, one clause (the main clause) is more important, and the other clause (the subordinate clause) depends on it, and cannot stand alone. Furthermore, the subordinate clause is often not a complete sentence.

There are several types of subordinate clauses in Pidgin (as in other languages): adverbial, infinitival, nominal, and relative. These are described in the following sections.

6.2.1 Adverbial clauses

Adverbial clauses are like adverbs in giving information about location, time, manner, etc. They are usually introduced by "subordinating conjunctions," such as *wen* (*when*), *bifo* (*befo, before*), and *kawz* (*coz, cause, because*). Here are some examples from Pidgin, presented in different categories with the subordinating conjunctions given. In the example sentences, the subordinate clause is underlined and the subordinating conjunction is in bold.

Time: *wen* (*when*), *wail* (*while*), *bifo* (*befo, before*), *aefta* (*after*)

*You neva notice someting funny **when she talk**?* (Kearns 2000:13)
'Didn't you notice something funny when she talked?'

*And **while he wipe his sweat** . . . , da spotters put on two more small weights . . .* (Lum 1999:22)
'And while he wiped his sweat . . . , the spotter put on two more small weights.'

*I get planny Latin vocabalery fo memorize **before I go sleep**.* (Kearns 2000:26)
'I have a lot of Latin vocabulary to memorize before I go to sleep.'

*I goin come back alive **afta I mahke**.* (DJB:51 [Matt.17:9])
'I'm going to come back alive after I die.'

Location: *wea* (*where*)

*Dey live ova dea **wea da dead peopo stay buried**.* (DJB:23 [Matt.8:28])
'They live over there where the dead people are buried.'

Purpose: *fo* (*for*)

*Everybody come **fo see dat house**.* (Lum 1990:92)
'Everybody comes to see that house.'

Reason: *kawz* (*coz, cause, because*)

*Russo tink he hot stuff **cause he stay in high school**.* (Lum 1999:20)
'Russo thinks he's hot stuff because he's in high school.'

Manner: *jalaik* (*j'like, jalike, just like*)

*God wen make um come back alive, **jalike Jesus wen say befo time**.* (DJB:93 [Matt.28:6])
'God made him come back alive, just like Jesus said earlier.'

Contrast: *do (though)*, *ivendo (even though)*

> *Anyways he look like one of da Russians **even though** he was Portogee.*
> (Lum 1999:24)
> 'Anyway, he looked like one of the Russians even though he was Portuguese.'

Conditional: *if*

> *But nowadays, **if** somebody no can read, everybody feega he stupid, too.* (Kearns 2000:21)
> "But nowadays if somebody can't read, everyone thinks he's stupid too.'

Negative conditional: *o els (or else),*

> *So you bettah behave **or else** I going come sit on you.*
> (Lum 1998b:229)
> 'So you'd better behave or else I'm going to come and sit on you.'

Negative contrast: *nomaeta (no matta, no matter)*

> *Mo betta you live foeva, **no matta** you no mo hand o leg.*
> (DJB:53 [Matt.18:8])
> 'It's better to live forever, even if you don't have hands or legs.'

6.2.2 Infinitival clauses

An infinitival clause is a subordinate clause that comes in the predicate, or second part of a sentence (after a verb or adjective). In English, it is usually introduced by the word *to*, as in *We tried to win the game*. In Pidgin, this type of clause is usually introduced by *fo (for)*:

> *My father said **for tell you**.* (Ching 1998:187)
> 'My father said to tell you.'

> *He ask me **fo cheer you up**.* (Kearns 2000:13)
> 'He asked me to cheer you up.'

*I neva have money **for** buy some mo.* (Yamanaka 1998b:155)
'I didn't have money to buy more.'

*He teach me how **fo** grip da bar.* (Lum 1999:22)
'He taught me how to grip the bar.'

*I wen try **fo** catch um.* (Chock 1998:29)
'I tried to catch it.'

*I too chicken **fo** say anyting.* (Lum 1998b:230)
'I was too chicken [scared] to say anything.'

Pidgin also has a type of infinitival clause not found in English. Here the clause functions as the second part of an equational (verbless) sentence, describing the subject or subjects by their habitual actions.

*Hr **fo** tawk enikain.*
(*Her **for** talk anykine.*)
'She's the kind who'd say anything.'

*Dem gaiz **fo** drink pleni.*
(*Dem guys **for** drink plenny.*)
'Those guys are heavy drinkers.'

6.2.3 Nominal clauses

A nominal clause is one that functions like a noun phrase in a sentence. For example, in the English sentence *I believe his explanation*, the NP "his explanation" is the object of the verb (i.e., what I believe). In the sentence *I believe he's telling the truth*, the clause "he's telling the truth" is the object (again, what I believe). Nominal clauses in English often begin with the complementizer *that*, as in *I believe that he's telling the truth*. In Pidgin, nominal clauses that act as objects are similar to those of English and usually begin with *daet* (*that*):

*All I can rememba is **dat** Latin no get one word order.*
(Kearns 2000:22)
'All I can remember is that Latin doesn't have a word order.'

*She tell me she pray **dat** Ah Goong stay okay.* (Lum 1998a:73)
'She told me she prays that Ah Goong is okay.'

In English, a nominal clause can also be the subject of a sentence, as in *That you'll pass the test is guaranteed* or *That we can't be there is very sad.* This type of nominal clause is not found in Pidgin. But in English, the word order of such clauses can be changed with an anticipatory subject, *it*: *It's guaranteed that you'll pass the test* and *It is very sad that we can't be there.* Similar nominal clauses are found in Pidgin, but the anticipatory *it* is not used, and neither is the linking verb or the complementizer—for example:

. . . garans he goin give you guys clotheses. (DJB:18 [Matt.6:30])
'. . . it's guaranteed that he'll give you all clothes.'

In Pidgin, the most common nominal clauses of this type follow *mobe-ta* (*mo betta, more better*):

Mo betta I stop now. (Kearns 2000:26)
'It's better if I stop now.'

Mo bettah he come play handball wit us. (Lum 1999:20-21)
'It's better if he comes to play handball with us.'

Mo betta, you put da grape juice inside one new kine leather bag. (DJB:26 [Matt/9:27])
'It's better if you put new wine in a new wineskin.'

6.2.4 Relative clauses

A relative clause further describes a noun or noun phrase. For example, compare these two sentences: *The woman plays basketball* and *The woman who works in our office plays basketball.* The relative clause *who works in our office* gives more information about the noun phrase *the woman.* The word *who* refers to *the woman*, and is called a "relative pronoun" or a "rela-tivizer." Other common relative pronouns in English include *which* and *that.* Pidgin also has relative clauses similar to those in English. The relative pronouns are *hu* (*who*) and *daet* (*dat, that*):

*He coach everybody **who** <u>come in da weightroom</u>.* (Lum 1999:22).
'He coached everybody who came to the weightroom.'

*Get one noddah girl **who** <u>no can stay still</u>.* (Kanae 1998:208)
'There's another girl who can't stay still.'

*Dey even had da funny kine gun **dat** <u>was fat at da end</u>.* (Lum 1998a:71)
'They even had the funny gun that was fat at the end.'

*He not jalike da teacha guys **dat** <u>teach God's Rules</u>.*
(DJB:20 [Matt.7:29])
'He's not like the teachers that teach God's Rules.'

There are two basic types of relative clauses. The sentence *The woman who works in our office plays basketball*, above, is an example of the first type. Here the noun phrase being described, *the woman*, is understood to be the subject of the relative clause—in other words, we understand that *the **woman** works in our office*, and the relative pronoun *who* refers to *the woman*. We'll call this type the "subject relative clause."

The following sentence has the second type of relative clause: *I didn't see the book that Lisa bought*. The relative clause *that Lisa bought* gives more information about *the book*. But here the noun phrase being described, *the book*, is understood to be the object of the relative clause—in other words, we understand that *Lisa bought **the book***, and that the relative pronoun *that* refers to *the book* even though it has been moved to the beginning of the relative clause. We'll call this type the "object relative clause."

With regard to object relative clauses, Pidgin and English are similar in that the relative pronoun can be omitted. So, for example:

*Ai neva si da buk **daet** <u>Lisa wen bai</u>.*
'I didn't see the book **that** <u>Lisa bought</u>.'

or

Ai neva si da buk <u>Lisa wen bai</u>.
'I didn't see the book <u>Lisa bought</u>.'

In fact, in Pidgin, the relative pronoun is not usually found in object relative clauses. Here are some more examples:

More betta you study dat SAT prep book <u>Auntie K wen loan you</u>.
(Kearns 2000:4)
'It's better if you study that SAT prep book Auntie K loaned you.'

Dis is dah bridge <u>we standing on right now</u>. (Pak 1998a:115)
'This is the bridge we're standing on right now.'

However, with regard to subject relative clauses, the two languages differ. First, the relative pronoun can be omitted in Pidgin but not in English:

You dah one <u>wen show us dah map</u>. (Pak 1998a:116)
'You're the one who showed us the map.'

I don't know anybody <u>study as much as you</u>. (Cataluna 2002:6)
'I don't know anybody who studies as much as you.'

Second, instead of using a relative pronoun in the relative clause, Pidgin can use a regular pronoun such as *hi* (*he*), *shi* (*she*), or *de* (*dey, they*):

*And get one skinny boy, **<u>he just stare at my braddah</u>**.* (Kanae 1998:208)
'And there was a skinny boy who just stared at my brother.'

*Aes da kain gaiz **de awl tawk onli**.*
'That's the kind of guys who are all talk, no action.'

6.3 Direct quotations

Direct quotations contain the exact words of what someone else said. In Pidgin, the quotation may be introduced by *sei* (*say*) or *sed* (*said*), but *tel* (*tell*) is the most common, especially in heavy Pidgin, and is often used where *say, said* or *ask* would be required in English:

*She **say**, "No drink too much milk . . . "* (Lum 1998b:225)
'She said, "Don't drink too much milk . . . " '

*He **said**, "You gotta put your mind to it."* (Lum 1999:19)
'He said, "You've got to put your mind to it." '

*Den one eye went pop open and he **tell**, "I was watching."*
(Lum 1999:26)
'Then one eye popped open and he said, "I was watching." '

*Den shi **tel**, "Wai yu no ask om?"*
'Then she said, "Why don't you ask him?" '

6.4 Sentences joined by connectors

"Connectors" are similar to conjunctions in that they are used to join two clauses together. The difference is that in this case, the clauses sometimes remain as separate sentences rather than being joined into a complex sentence.

Sequence: *den (then), aen den (an then, and then)*:

*. . . we saw dah piece pepah on dah ground. **Den** I pick 'em up and was dah map.* (Pak 1998a:102)
' . . . we saw the piece of paper on the ground. Then I picked it up and it was the map.'

*Fo' long time wuz quiet. **Den** she wen ax me one weird question.*
(Tonouchi 1998:249)
'For a long time it was quiet. Then she asked me a weird question.'

*. . . you gotta stand still fo at least one second before you can let um go. **And den**, dey jes drop um on da floor . . .* (Lum 1999:21)
' . . . you've got to stand still for at least one second before you can let it go. And then they just drop it on the floor . . . '

Consequence: *so*:

*Had plenny guys standing around da door **so** I jes went squeeze by dem.* (Lum 1999:24)
'There were a lot of guys standing around the door, so I just squeezed by them.'

My mouth was all watery cause I like eat um all one time, eh? **So** *I wen'
tell her, Gimme that bag.* (Yamanaka 1998a:153)
'My mouth was all watery because I wanted to eat them all at once, you
know. So I told her, Gimme that bag.'

My little braddah, he not mento. **So** *you bettah stop teasing him.*
(Kanae 1998:208)
'My brother isn't mental. So you'd better stop teasing him.'

Negative conditional: *bambai* (*bumbye, by 'm by*):

(Note that this is a different usage from when *bambai* [*bumbye, by 'm
by*] is used as an adverb indicating future time [section 3.10].)

Yu beta teik yaw ambrela. **Bambai** *yu get wet.*
'You'd better take your umbrella. Otherwise you'll get wet.'

No get da tomatoes wet, **bumbye** *going get spots.* (Lum 1998b:225)
Don't get the tomatoes wet, otherwise they're going to get spots.'

No be like Anakin, **bumbye** *you become Darth Vader.* (Kearns 2000:14)
'Don't be like Anakin; otherwise you'll become Darth Vader.'

**Cause or result: *aeswai* (*ass why*), *daeswai* (*das why, dass why, that's
why*):**

This is one of the most common connectors in Pidgin. Note that it can
come at the beginning or at the end of a sentence. When it comes at the
beginning of a sentence, that sentence is the result and the preceding sentence is the cause:

Ai neva stadi. **Aeswai** *ai wen flank.*
'I didn't study. That's why I flunked.'

Kennet when he fight, he always try his best. **Das why** *he win.*
(Lum 1998b:227)
'When Kennet fights, he always tries his best. That's why he wins.'

When it comes at the end of a sentence, that sentence is the cause and the preceding sentence is the result.

Shi no laik kam klos. Shi ste wail **aeswai**.
'She doesn't like to come close because she's wild.'

Stay ova dea till I tell you fo come back. King Herod, he goin look fo da boy fo kill him, **dass why**. (DJB:4 [Matt.2.13])
'Stay over there till I tell you to come back because King Herod is going to look for the boy to kill him.'

Conclusion

The preceding chapters of this book have provided only a preliminary sketch of Pidgin grammar. This means that many details of the language have not been covered here. Also, there are some other aspects of Pidgin that have not been covered because they need further study. These are briefly outlined below, followed by a short discussion of the issue of the use of Pidgin in education.

Further study

One aspect of Pidgin that needs further study is the question of variation in Pidgin. This involves gaining further understanding of the differences between heavy and light Pidgin, and who speaks what kind of Pidgin and in what circumstances. It also involves the question of regional dialects. Many people talk about Big Island Pidgin, Kaua'i Pidgin, and even Kalihi Pidgin, and there are some words or expressions that are used mostly in one location as opposed to others. For example, on the Big Island, people say *ice shave* rather than *shave ice*. On Maui, people use *sam* (*some*) as a degree modifier (section 3.6) more frequently than on other islands. And the use of *haed* (*had*) as a past tense marker (3.8.2) often identifies the speaker as coming from Kaua'i. But the extent of regional differences has not been studied, especially in the prosodic aspects of language, such as intonation. This would be a very interesting topic of research.

Another question concerns the influence of other languages on the pronunciation of Pidgin, as mentioned in the first chapter (section 1.2.5). For example, many people think that the vowel sounds of Pidgin are similar to those of Portuguese, and that the intonation in questions is similar to that of Hawaiian. But again, this has not been studied in any detail.

Finally, there is the question of how Pidgin is changing. Is it becoming more like standard English, as some people think, or is it becoming more like vernacular varieties, such as African-American Vernacular English (Ebonics)?

Pidgin in the classroom

Some of the questions just mentioned would be interesting topics for discussion in classrooms in Hawai'i. But even though Pidgin is an important part of local culture and identity in Hawai'i, it is most often ignored or avoided in the educational process. We believe that this should change. Of course, we are **not** suggesting that Pidgin should be taught in the classroom, or that it should be the language used for instruction. But we do think that learning about Pidgin is very important.

First of all, education involves learning about your history and environment. Students in Hawai'i learn about the history of the islands and about the local geography. Since Pidgin is a significant part of local culture, they should learn about its origins, and understand that it is a legitimate language variety, not "bad English."

Second, an important goal of education is to learn standard English. Since Pidgin has always been considered an obstacle to this goal, it has been virtually banned from the classroom. But learning about Pidgin can actually be a valuable tool for learning standard English. Often, students who speak Pidgin do not recognize how it differs from English. By studying the structure of their language, they can focus on the differences that exist in standard English.

The best way for students to learn that Pidgin is a legitimate rule-governed variety of language, and to see how it compares with English, is for them to analyze their own language and discover for themselves its grammatical patterns or "rules." Teachers can demonstrate that there are grammatical rules in Pidgin (for example, that it doesn't sound right to say *we wen saw dat movie already*). Then they can ask students to think about a particular grammatical area in Pidgin, such as negatives, and see what subconscious rules there are for what speakers can and cannot say, and how these rules differ from those of standard English.

Thus, while this book would be useful for college students studying about Pidgin, it is not meant to be used as a textbook for primary, intermediate, or high school students. Rather, it is meant to be a resource for teachers of these students—to find out about the origins of Pidgin, and to use as a guide for checking their students' grammatical intuitions or explaining subtle differences between Pidgin and standard English.

A Pidgin Word List

This list contains Pidgin words derived from English that have different meanings or functions, and words derived from other languages. For some words, the section numbers are given where the meanings or functions are described in the preceding chapters. To help people unfamiliar with the Odo orthography, most English-derived words are given in English spelling, with the Odo spelling sometimes following in square brackets. Where the word is given in Odo orthography, other English spellings are given in parentheses.

act [aek]. Show off.

adobo. Filipino dish with pork or chicken cooked in vinegar and garlic.

after [aefta]. After; afterwards.

ahi. Tuna (Hawaiian *'ahi*).

akamai. Smart (Hawaiian).

aks [aeks]. Ask. Also **aes (as)**.

ala-alas. Testicles (Hawaiian *'alā'alā* 'small, dense, waterworn volcanic stones').

alas. See *ala-alas*.

ali'i. Chief or Hawaiian noble (Hawaiian).

aloha. Love; affection; compassion; a greeting (Hawaiian).

aloha shirt. Shirt with colorful tropical print.

alphabet [aelfabet]. Letter of the alphabet; alphabet.

already [awredi]. Already; indicates that an action or state has come to pass.

anykine [enikain]. Many kinds of.

anyways [eniweiz]. Anyway.

arare [aDaDe]. Japanese rice crackers (Japanese).

ass [aes]. That's (3.3.2, 5.4.1).

ass why [aeswai]. That's why (6.4).

au au. Bath (Hawaiian *'au'au* 'bathe').

auwe. Oh! Alas! (Hawaiian *auē*).

babooz [babuz]. Idiot (Portuguese *babosa* 'stupid, simpleton').

bachi. Punishment; retribution (Japanese).

bago-ong, bagoong. Filipino fermented fish sauce (Tagalog).

bakatare. Fool; idiot (Japanese).

balut/balot. Chicken egg with a partly formed embryo (Filipino languages).

bambucha. Big thing; largest size marble (origin unknown, possibly a dialect of Portuguese).

beef [bif]. Fight (verb).

bafe [beif]. Bathe.

befo time [bifo taim]. Earlier; in the past.

benjo. Toilet (Japanese).

bento. Japanese-style box lunch (Japanese).

bin. Past tense marker (3.8.2).

blala. Brother.

bobura. Person born in Japan; pumpkin head (Japanese, from Portuguese *abobora* 'pumpkin; weak man').

bocha. Bath; bathe (western Japanese).

boddah [bada]. Bother.

bolohead [bolohed]. Bald (*bald* + *head*).

born [bawn]. Give birth to.

boro(s) [boDo(s)]. See *boroboro(s)*.

boroboro(s) [boDoboDo]. Old worn-out clothes (Japanese *boroboro* 'rags').

brah [bra]. Brother.

broke [brok]. Break; tear; broken; tore; torn.

broke da mouth [brok da maut]. Very delicious!

buckaloose [bakalus]. Break loose; go out of control.

buddha-head [buda-hed]. Local person of Japanese ancestry.

buggah [baga]. Guy.

bukbuk. Flashy Filipino person (Filipino languages, words for certain kinds of insects).

bulai. To tell lies (*bull* + *lie*).

bumboocha. See *bambucha*.

bumbye [bambai]. Later (3.10); otherwise (6.4).

bus [bas]. Break.

bus up [bas ap]. Beat up.

buta kaukau. Pig food; pig slop (Japanese *buta* 'pig'; Pidgin *kaukau* 'food').

cat tongue. Unable to drink or eat hot things.

catch air [kaech ea]. Breathe.

catch head [kaech hed]. Take advantage.

catch him up [kaech om ap]. Catch up to him.

chance 'em [chaens om]. Take a chance.

char siu. Barbequed pork (Chinese languages).

chawan cut [chawan kat]. Haircut in the shape of an inverted rice bowl (Japanese *chawan* 'rice bowl').

chichi(s). Breast(s) (Japanese *chichi* 'milk').

chicken skin [chiken skin]. Goose bumps.

chocho lips. Small, butterfly-shaped lips (Japanese *chocho* 'butterfly').

choke [chok]. Very many; a lot of.

chrai. Try; politeness marker (5.7).

cockaroach [kakaroch]. Steal or sneak away with.

come [kam]. Come; become.

crack seed [kraeksid]. Chinese tangy snacks.

cut neck [kat nek]. Lost one's job; fired.

da. The (3.3.1).

da kine [da kain]. (See section 3.15.)

daikon. Kind of turnip (Japanese).

daikon legs. White, short, fat legs (Japanese *daikon* 'a kind of turnip').

dakain (da kine). The kind of; of these/those; whachamacallit.

dass [daes]. That's (3.3.2, 5.4.1).

dass why [daeswai]. That's why (6.4).

dat [daet]. That.

de (dey). They.

dem. Them; postmodifier (3.12).

dis. This.

dono. I don't know.

ehu. Reddish brown (of hair color) (Hawaiian *'ehu*).

every time [evritaim]. All the time; always.

figga [figa]. Think.

figure. See *figga*.

fo. For; to (6.2.2).

from long time [fram lawng taim]. For a long time.

garans [gaerenz]. Guaranteed.

get. Get; have; existential (5.2).

girigiri [giDigiDi]. Cowlick; or the spot on the back of the head where the skull shows through the hair (Japanese *guriguri*).

give 'em! [giv om!]. Give 'em hell.

go for broke [go fo brok]. Go all out.

gon (goin, going). Future tense marker (3.8.1, 4.5.2.1).

goza. Straw mat (Japanese).

grind [grain]. Eat.

grinds [grainz]. Food.

guys [gaiz]. People; plural marker (3.2); postmodifier (3.12).

habut. Pout (Japanese *habuteru*).

had [haed]. Past tense marker (3.8.2); past tense existential (5.2).

hale. House; building (Hawaiian).

hana. Work (Hawaiian).

hana hou. Do it again (Hawaiian).

hanabata. Snot (Japanese *hana* 'nose'; *bata* from English *butter*).

hanabata days. The carefree days of childhood (*hanabata* 'snot').

hanahana. Work (Hawaiian *hana*).

hanai. Adopted (Hawaiian *hānai* 'foster child').

hanau. Give birth (Hawaiian *hānau*).

haole. White person (Hawaiian).

haolefied. Become like a *haole*.

hapa. Half; mixed race (Hawaiian, from English *half*).

hapai. Carry; pregnant (Hawaiian *hāpai*).

hard rub [had rab]. Close competition.

hashi. Chopsticks (Japanese).

haupia. Coconut cream pudding (Hawaiian).

heiau. Pre-Christian religious site (Hawaiian).

hele. Go; come; move; walk (Hawaiian).

hele on. Move on (Hawaiian *hele* 'go; come; move').

hemajang [haemajaeng]. All mixed up (origin unknown).

hemo. Remove; loose (Hawaiian).

hibachi. Charcoal grill (Japanese).

high makamaka [hai makamaka]. Pretentious; important person.

hilahila. Shy; ashamed (Hawaiian).

ho. Man! (Hawaiian *hō*).

holoholo. Go for a walk (Hawaiian).

honu. Turtle (Hawaiian).

how much [hau mach]. How much; how many.

how you figga [hau yu figa]. How did that happen?!

howzit [hauzit]. Greeting: how are you?

huhu. Angry; offended (Hawaiian *huhū*).

hui. Club, organization (Hawaiian).

hula. Hawaiian dance (Hawaiian).

hula halau. Hula dance group (Hawaiian *hālau* 'long house for *hula* instruction').

huli. Turn over; flip (Hawaiian).

hulihuli chicken. Chicken barbecued on a spit (Hawaiian *huli* 'to turn').

hybolic. Using fancy (or standard-sounding) language (from English *hyperbolic* [?]).

imu. Earth oven (Hawaiian).

in front [infran]. In front of.

inside [insaid, insai]. Inside of; in.

jalike, j'like [jalaik]. Just like.

janken po. Paper, scissors and stone game (Japanese *jan ken pon*).

junk [jank]. Junk; not good; terrible.

karai [kaDai]. Salty; spicy hot (Japanese).

kahuna. Priest; expert (Hawaiian).

kala. Money (Hawaiian *kālā* from English *dollar*).

kalako. Multicolored; variegated in color (Hawaiian *kalakoa* from English *calico*).

kalua pig. Pig baked in a ground oven (Hawaiian *kālua* 'bake in ground oven').

kama'aina. Person born in Hawai'i or long-term resident (Hawaiian *kama'āina*).

kamaboko [kamabuko]. Kind of fish cake (Japanese).

kapakahi. Crooked; inside out; mixed up (Hawaiian).

kapu. Taboo (Hawaiian).

karang [karaeng]. Bang; hit; twist.

katonk, kotonk. Japanese person from the mainland (origin unknown).

katsu. Cultlet (Japanese) e.g., chicken katsu.

kaukau. Food; eat (Chinese Pidgin English).

kay den [ke daen]. OK then (giving in to someone).

keiki. Child; children (Hawaiian).

kiawe. Algaroba tree (Hawaiian).

kimchee [kimchi]. Spicy pickled cabbage (Korean).

kine [kain]. Kind (3.15); postmodifier (3.12).

kini. Small marble (originally made of metal) (Hawaiian, from English *tin*).

koa. Kind of native forest tree (Hawaiian).

kokua. Help (Hawaiian *kōkua*).

kolohe. Mischievous; naughty; comic; prankster (Hawaiian).

kukae [kukai]. Excrement (Hawaiian *kūkae*).

kukui nuts [kukui nats]. Candlenuts (Hawaiian *kukui* 'candlenut tree').

kuleana [kuliana]. Responsibility (Hawaiian).

lanai. Verandah (Hawaiian *lānai*).

laters [leitaz]. See you later.

laulau. Meat or taro tops cooked in ti leaves (Hawaiian).

lavalava. Sarong (Samoan).

lawnmower [lawnmowa]. Mow (e.g., *lawnmower the grass*); lawnmower.

lei. Flower garland (Hawaiian).

lickens [likinz]. A beating (especially *dirty lickins*).

lidat, li'dat [laidaet]. And things like that (3.15).

li hing mui. Salty, sour dried plum (Chinese languages).

like [laik]. Want to; like (3.9).

lilibit. See *litobit*.

lilikoi. Passionfruit (Hawaiian *liliko'i*).

limu. Kind of edible seaweed (Hawaiian).

litobit [liDobit]. A little; less (3.4).

local, loco [lokol]. From Hawai'i.

lolo. Stupid; crazy (Hawaiian *lōlō*).

lomilomi. Massage (Hawaiian *lomi*).

lomilomi salmon. Diced tomatoes and onions with salt salmon (Hawaiian *lomi* 'rub; crush').

lua. Toilet (Hawaiian *lua* 'hole').

luau. Hawaiian feast (Hawaiian *lū'au*).

luau feet [luau fit]. Big feet (Hawaiian *lu'au* 'taro leaf').

luna. Plantation overseer (Hawaiian *luna* 'above').

mahalo. Thank you (Hawaiian).

mahimahi. Dolphin fish (Hawaiian).

mahu. Transvestite (Hawaiian *māhū*).

makai. Toward the sea (Hawaiian *ma kai*).

ma-ke, mahke [make]. Die (Hawaiian *make*).

make [mek]. Make; do.

make 'A' [mek 'A']. See *make ass*.

make ass [mek aes]. Make a fool of oneself; goof up.

makule. Old (Hawaiian).

malassada. Holeless doughnut (Portuguese).

manapua. Chinese bun (Hawaiian *mea 'ono pua'a* 'delicious pork thing').

manini. Stingy; undersized (Hawaiian).

manong. Brother (to Filipinos); Filipino guy (to non-Filipinos).

mauka. Toward the mountains (Hawaiian *ma uka*).

mele. Chant or song (Hawaiian).

menehune. Legendary race of small people (Hawaiian).

menpachi [mempachi]. Small snapper (fish) with big eyes (Japanese).

menpachi eyes [mempachi aiz]. Big eyes.

mento. Mental; insane.

mo. More; degree modifier (3.6).

mo betta [mo beta]. Better.

mo litobit [mo liDobit]. Less; fewer (3.6).

mo worse [mo wrs]. Worse.

mochi. Rice patty (Japanese).

moemoe. Sleep; lie down (Hawaiian).

moke [mok]. Tough local man (Hawaiian *moko* 'fighter').

monku [mongku]. Complain; grumble (Japanese).

musubi. Rice ball (western Japanese).

muumuu. Loose-fitting long dress (Hawaiian *muʻumuʻu*).

nene. Hawaiian goose (Hawaiian *nēnē*).

never [neva]. Didn't; past tense negative marker (5.6).

niele. Inquisitive; nosy (Hawaiian *niele*).

no matta [nomaeta]. Even if (6.2.1).

noda [nada]. Another; other.

nomo. Isn't/aren't any; doesn't/don't have (5.6).

nori [noDi]. Dried seaweed (Japanese).

nuff [naf]. Enough.

obake. Ghost (Japanese).

off [awf]. Off; turn off (e.g., *off the light*).

ohana. Extended family (Hawaiian *ʻohana*).

okole. Buttocks (Hawaiian *ʻōkole* 'anus').

om ('em). Him; her; it (3.2).

on top [awntap]. On top of; on.

onaga. Ruby snapper (Japanese).

one [wan]. One; a; an (3.3.1).

one other [wan ada]. Another.

ono. Delicious (Hawaiian *ʻono*).

onolicious [onolishes]. Delicious (Hawaiian *ʻono*).

opae. Shrimp (Hawaiian *ʻōpae*).

opala. Trash; rubbish (Hawaiian *ʻōpala*).

opihi. Limpet (Hawaiian *ʻopihi*).

opu. Stomach; belly (Hawaiian *ʻōpū*).

package [paekej]. Sack; paper bag; package.

pakalolo. Marijuana (Hawaiian *paka lōlō*).

pake. Chinese (Hawaiian *pākē*).

pali. Cliff (Hawaiian).

paniolo. Cowboy (Hawaiian, from Spanish *español* 'Spanish').

panty [paenti]. Panty; sissy; weakling.

pāo doce. Sweet bread (Portuguese).

pau. Finish; finished (Hawaiian *pau* 'finished'); completive auxiliary (4.5.2.3).

pau hana. Quitting time; retirement (Hawaiian).

pear [pea]. Avocado; pear.

peopo, peopol [pipo, pipol]. People.

pikake. Jasmine plant (Hawaiian *pīkake*).

piko. Navel (Hawaiian).

pilau. Dirty (Hawaiian *pilau* 'rotten').

pilikia. Trouble; bother (Hawaiian).

pine [pain]. Pineapple; pine.

planny, plenny, plenty [plaeni, pleni]. A lot of; many; much.

poha. Cape gooseberry (Hawaiian *pohā*).

poho. Loss; wasted effort; useless (Hawaiian *pohō*).

poi. Pounded taro (Hawaiian).

poi dog. Mixed breed dog (Hawaiian *poi* 'pounded taro').

poke. Cubed raw or cooked seafood salad (Hawaiian *poke* 'slice; cut').

popolo. Black; African American (Hawaiian *pōpolo*).

potagee [poDogi]. Portuguese.

pressure out [praesha aut]. Get totally stressed out.

puka. Hole (Hawaiian).

pupu(s). Party snacks; finger food (Hawaiian *pūpū*).

pupule. Crazy; insane (Hawaiian).

pupule house [pupule haus]. Mental institution (Hawaiian *pupule* 'insane').

puries [pyuriz]. Clear marbles.

saimin. Japanese broth with noodles (Chinese languages).

salty [sawlti]. Salty; angry.

sashimi. Sliced raw fish (Japanese).

shaka. Right on!; great; hand signal with several meanings (from English *shocker*).

shame [sheim]. Shy; bashful; embarrassing.

shave ice [shevais]. Shaved ice with flavored syrup, like a snowcone.

shibai. Ruse; playacting (Japanese).

shishi. Urine; urinate (Japanese *oshikko*).

shoyu. Soy sauce (Japanese).

side [said]. Side; postmodifier (3.12).

skebei. Dirty old man (Japanese *sukebei*).

skosh/skoshi. A little bit (Japanese *sukoshi*).

slippers [slipaz]. Rubber thongs; flipflops.

small kid time. Childhood.

some [sam]. Some; really; very (3.6).

spark, spahk [spak]. Spot (someone or something); check out.

spesho. Special.

start [stat]. Start; inchoative auxiliary (4.5.2.3).

ste (stay, stei). Am/is/are/was/were; auxiliary indicating progressive or perfective (4.5.2.3).

stink eye [stink ai]. Dirty look.

tako. Octopus (Japanese).

talk stink [tawk stink]. Say bad things about someone.

talk story [tawk stawri]. Have informal conversation; tell stories; gossip.

tantaran [tantaDan]. Crazy; grandstanding; putting on airs (Western Japanese *taran* 'not enough,' reinforced by Filipino tarantá).

tell [tel]. Say; tell (6.3).

thinkso [tinkso]. Think (something) (from Chinese Pidgin English).

throw act [chrou aek]. Put on an act; throw a tantrum.

throw out [chrou aut]. Throw up; vomit.

time [taim]. Time; postmodifier (3.12).

tita. Tough local woman (from English *sister* via Hawaiian).

too much [tumach]. Too much; too many.

try [chrai]. Try (4.5.2.2); politeness marker in commands (5.7).

tsunami. Tidal wave (Japanese).

tutu. Grandma; grandpa (Hawaiian *kūkū*).

uku. Louse (Hawaiian *'uku*); very many.

uku million [uku milyan]. Many millions.

uku plenty [uku pleni]. A lot of; very very many.

ume. Partially dried salted sour plum pickle (Japanese).

unagi. Eel (Japanese).

wahine. Woman (Hawaiian).

wan (one). One; a; an (3.3.1).

wan bok [wan bak]. Kind of Chinese cabbage (Chinese languages).

wen. Past tense marker (3.8.2, 4.5.2.1).

what fo [watfo]. Why? For what reason?

whatevahs [watevaz]. Whatever; it doesn't matter.

yustu (used to). Past habitual tense marker (3.8.3).

zori(s). Thong(s); flipflop(s) (Japanese).

References

Bickerton, Derek. 1977. *Change and Variation in Hawaiian English. Volume II. Creole Syntax.* (Final report on National Science Foundation Grant no. GS-39748). Honolulu: Social Sciences and Linguistics Institute, University of Hawai'i.

Bickerton, Derek, and Carol Odo. 1976. *Change and Variation in Hawaiian English. Volume I. General Phonology and Pidgin Syntax.* (Final report on National Science Foundation Grant no. GS-39748). Honolulu: Social Sciences and Linguistics Institute, University of Hawai'i.

Bickerton, Derek, and William H. Wilson. 1987. Pidgin Hawaiian. In Glenn G. Gilbert, (ed.), *Pidgin and Creole Languages: Essays in Memory of John E. Reinecke.* Honolulu: University of Hawai'i Press, 61–76.

Bond, Kathryn L. 1937. We'll go see the world. In Willard Wilson (ed.), *College Plays, Volume I.* Typescript. Hamilton Library, University of Hawai'i at Mānoa, 85–96.

bradajo [Joseph Hadley]. 1998a. ma ket stenlei. In Eric Chock et al. (eds.), *Growing Up Local,* 19–26.

———. 1998b.feescol ajukeshen. In Eric Chock et al. (eds.), *Growing Up Local,* 167–172.

Carr, Elizabeth Ball. 1972. *Da Kine Talk: From Pidgin to Standard English in Hawaii.* Honolulu: University of Hawai'i Press.

Cataluna, Lee. 2002. *Super Secret Squad.* Honolulu: Kumu Kahua Theatre.

Ching, Stuart. 1998. Way back to Palolo. In Eric Chock et al. (eds.), *Growing Up Local,* 180–190.

Chock, Eric. 1998. Da glove. In Eric Chock et al. (eds.), *Growing Up Local,* 28–29.

Chock, Eric, James R. Harstad, Darrell H. Y. Lum and Bill Teter (eds.). 1998. *Growing up Local: An Anthology of Poetry and Prose from Hawai'i.* Honolulu: Bamboo Ridge.

Da Jesus Book. 2000. *Da Jesus Book* [Hawai'i Pidgin New Testament]. Orlando: Wycliffe Bible Translators.

Kanae, Lisa Linn. 1998. Short tongue. In Eric Chock et al. (eds.), *Growing Up Local,* 208–209.

Kearns, Yokanaan. 2000. *Pidg Latin and How Kitty Got Her Pidgin Back.* Honolulu: Honolulu Theatre for Youth & Kumu Kahua Theatre.

Kono, Juliet S. 1998. A scolding from my father. In Eric Chock et al. (eds.), *Growing Up Local,* 210–211.

Labov, William. 1990. On the adequacy of natural languages: I. The development of tense. In John V. Singler (ed.), *Pidgin and Creole Tense-Mood-Aspect Systems.* Amsterdam/Philadelphia: John Benjamins, 1–58.

Lum, Darrell H. Y. 1990. *Pass On, No Pass Back!* Honolulu: Bamboo Ridge Press.

———. 1998a. Giving tanks. In Eric Chock et al. (eds.), *Growing Up Local,* 71–74.

———. 1998b. Orphan Annie: Coloring in the eyes. In Eric Chock et al. (eds.), *Growing Up Local,* 222–231.

———. 1999. YMCA: The weightroom. In John R. Rickford and Suzanne Romaine (eds.), *Creole Genesis, Attitudes and Discourse: Studies Celebrating Charlene J. Sato.*

Amsterdam/Philadelphia: John Benjamins, 19–27.

Masuda, Barry. 1998. No mo' fish on Maui. In E. Chock et al. (eds.), *Growing Up Local*, 232.

Masuda, Hirokuni. 2000. *The Genesis of Discourse Grammar: Universals and Substrata in Guyanese, Hawaii Creole, and Japanese*. New York: Peter Lang.

Morales, Rodney. 1988. *The Speed of Darkness*. Honolulu: Bamboo Ridge Press.

Odo, Carol. 1975. *Phonological Processes in the English Dialect of Hawaii*. Ph.D. dissertation, University of Hawai'i.

———. 1977. Phonological representations in Hawaiian English. *University of Hawaii Working Papers in Linguistics* 9(3): 77–85.

Pak, Gary. 1998a. The gift. In Eric Chock et al. (eds.), *Growing Up Local*, 98–119.

———. 1998b. The valley of the dead air. In Eric Chock et al. (eds.), *Growing Up Local*, 319–327.

Perlman, Alan M. 1973. *Grammatical Structure and Style-shift in Hawaiian Pidgin and Creole*. Ph.D. dissertation, University of Chicago.

Reinecke, John. 1969. *Language and Dialect in Hawaii: A Sociolinguistic History to 1935*. Honolulu: University of Hawai'i Press.

Roberts, Julian M. 1993. The transformation of Hawaiian plantation pidgin and the emergence of Hawaii Creole English. Paper presented at Annual Conference of the Society for Pidgin and Creole Lingusitics, Amsterdam, June.

———. 1995. Pidgin Hawaiian: A sociohistorical study. *Journal of Pidgin and Creole Languages* 10: 1–56.

Roberts, Sarah J. 1998. The role of diffusion in the genesis of Hawaiian Creole. *Language* 74: 1–39.

———. Nativization and genesis of Hawaiian creole. In John H. McWhorter (ed.), *Language Change and Language Contact in Pidgins and Creoles*. Amsterdam/Philadelphia: John Benjamins, 257–300.

Sato, Charlene J. 1989. A nonstandard approach to standard English. *TESOL Quarterly* 23: 259–282.

———. 1991. Sociolinguistic variation and attitudes in Hawaii. In Jenny Cheshire (ed.), *English Around the World: Sociolinguistic Perspectives*. Cambridge: Cambridge University Press, 647–663.

Siegel, Jeff. 2000. Substrate influence in Hawai'i Creole English. *Language in Society* 29: 197–236.

Simonson, Douglas (Peppo), Ken Sakata, and Pat Sasaki. 1981. *Pidgin to da Max*. Honolulu: Bess Press.

Simonson, Douglas, Ken Sakata, Pat Sasaki, and Todd Kurosawa. 1982. *Pidgin to da Max Hana Hou*. Honolulu: Bess Press.

Tonouchi, Lee A. 1998. Where to put your hands. In Eric Chock et al. (eds.), *Growing Up Local*, 245–252.

———. 2001. *Da Word*. Honolulu: Bamboo Ridge Press.

Vanderslice, Ralph, and Laura Shun Pierson. 1967. Prosodic features of Hawaiian English. *Quarterly Journal of Speech* 53: 156–166.

Yamanaka, Lois-Ann. 1998a. Boss of the food. In Eric Chock et al. (eds.), *Growing Up Local*, 153–154.

———. 1998b. Lickens. In Eric Chock et al. (eds.), *Growing Up Local*, 155–156.

Index